A Little Book of
American Humorous Verse

A
Little Book of
American Humorous Verse

Compiled by

T. A. Daly, *1871-1948, comp,*

Granger Index Reprint Series

 BOOKS FOR LIBRARIES PRESS
FREEPORT, NEW YORK

First Published 1926
Reprinted 1972

INTERNATIONAL STANDARD BOOK NUMBER:
0-8369-6329-6

LIBRARY OF CONGRESS CATALOG CARD NUMBER:
73-38597

PRINTED IN THE UNITED STATES OF AMERICA
BY
NEW WORLD BOOK MANUFACTURING CO., INC.
HALLANDALE, FLORIDA 33009

TO

ALL LOVERS

OF

THE LAUGHING MUSE

PREFACE

THIS little book of light verse set out originally to be a bigger and more ambitious thing. It was my hope to make it a complete compilation of the full treasury of humorous verse (made in America) since the earliest troubadour, lifting his voice in English, first began to carol merrily in this New World.

Such a volume, so far as I knew, or still know, has never been attempted. There have been many American anthologies, but none devoted solely to humorous verse or covering the whole range of that body of light song. Even more numerous have been the humorous anthologies in which the work of American poets has been included, but in most of these the majority of the singers represented are native to the soil of England. Some day The Complete Book of American Humorous Verse must be given to an expectant, patriotic people. Indeed, yes; but this cannot be it.

The patient and precise scholar, the true anthologist, who will eventually perform that great and necessary task, will delve into long-forgotten tomes, not now easily accessible, and rescue from dark and dusty recesses the

PREFACE

lyric jests of yesteryear. Or, failing that, he will at
least make plain to us why such things never were. I
was surprised and not a little discomfited to find, in my
casual research, so little American verse bearing date of
manufacture earlier than 1800 that could, by any stretch
of fancy or fond partisanship, be called even mildly
humorous. England, in the last half of the Seventeenth
and all of the Eighteenth Century, was uncommonly
rich in comic poets, and Grub Street enjoyed its heyday
of rollicking song. Why, at the same time, was there
such dearth of gay singing here? There are several and
doubtless correct explanations.

America had, before 1800, few poets of any sort; and
it may be supposed that their audience, the general pub-
lic, was so deeply engaged in the serious business, first, of
winning the wilderness and, later, of building up the
Republic that it had no time for frivolity. Yet it is
inconceivable that the Colonies were utterly lacking in
original and irrepressible spirits doubly gifted with
humor and song. Some anthologist may yet seek them
out, and it is my modest hope that to such a man this
present little experiment may serve as spur and guide.
To that end I have made the scheme of this book such
as I believe that greater work—when it comes—must
follow.

PREFACE

Here, then, is a small compilation, not a complete collection, of humorous verse of strictly American make. The "makers" (as all poets were once called) are arranged as nearly as possible in the order of their birth —and right here, for all my harping upon the American note, I must acknowledge my debt to the great British anthologist, Sir Arthur Quiller-Couch, whose Oxford Book of English Verse has been my own guide in the mechanics of this. There is one advantage in this chronological arrangement. For, while it discloses the pitiful paucity of material produced before the Nineteenth Century, it shows the gradual changes in popular taste and the steady increase of gayety and variety in the work of the later followers of the Comic Muse.

It must be admitted, however, that by the test of continued popularity (which is as much as to say by the judgment of time) the gentle "Autocrat of the Breakfast Table," Dr. Oliver Wendell Holmes, who was our first truly humorous poet, is still a leader among his fellows. Several of those who precede him in these pages were his equals in the art of high song, but none approached him in lyric humor. The man whose name is given first place in this book, Edward Bangs, is almost a myth (we know only that he flourished about 1776), and the solitary selection credited to him is the merest

PREFACE

doggerel. Yet I make no apology for giving the place of honor to "Yankee Doodle," for though it is no longer a national song it is still a national air and has been so for 150 years.

Here, also, it serves to accentuate the dominant note of this book of Yankee notions. It would be impossible, as I have said before, to give place to all the humorous verse-writers of America. Where the bulk, if not the wealth, of material is so great, it is the necessity as well as the office of the anthologist to pick and choose sparingly. In any choice, of course, personal bias cannot help but figure; and so there will be critics to object to what they may be pleased to call my sins of omission— and of admission, too, perhaps.

There have been, I doubt not, unintentional omissions of verses I would have wished to include, but there are other omissions that have been deliberate. I have denied place to parody, burlesque and those selections which, being merely comic or clever, did not measure up to my notion of truly humorous verse. Some names will be missed in these pages that should be in them. The fault is not mine nor that of the publisher, who fully approved my insistence that the rights and demands of individual authors must be respected.

I have my favorites, to be sure; but it is my hope

PREFACE

that I have managed to bring together here most of the
favorites of the contemporary public. Above all things,
I have sought to include those writers who seem to me
to have struck a distinctively American note in their
contributions to the treasury of humor in English verse
—English! how that word persists in bobbing up, to
flout our boast of exclusive Americanism! I have al-
ready made a grateful salaam to Quiller-Couch, and I
must turn now to another English poet and scholar for
the words which best describe the contents of this little
book. Whatever else may be said of them, most of the
selections admitted to these pages, I think, contain at
least a spark of the lyric fire of which the late Austin
Dobson sang:

> Oh, the Song where not one of the Graces
>   Tight-laces,—
> Where we woo the sweet Muses not starchly
>   But archly,—
>
> Where the verse, like a piper a-Maying,
>   Comes playing,—
> And the rhyme is as gay as a dancer
>   In answer,—
>
> It will last till men weary of pleasure
>   In measure!
> It will last till men weary of laughter.
>   And after!

EDWARD BANGS (?)

Yankee Doodle

(Flourished 1776)

FATHER and I went down to camp,
  Along with Captain Goodwin,
Where we see the men and boys
  As thick as Hasty-puddin.

There was captain Washington
  Upon a slapping stallion,
A giving orders to his men—
  I guess there was a million.

And then the feathers on his hat,
  They looked so tarnal fina,
I wanted pockily to get
  To give to my Jemima.

And there they had a swampin gun
  As large as log of maple,
On a deuced little cart—
  A load for father's cattle;

And every time they fired it off,
  It took a horn of powder;
It made a noise like father's gun,
  Only a nation louder.

I went as near to it myself
  As Jacob's underpinnin,
And father went as near again—
  I thought the deuce was in him.

And there I see a little keg,
  Its heads were made of leather—
They knocked upon't with little sticks
  To call the folks together.

EDWARD BANGS

And there they'd fife away like fun,
   And play on cornstock fiddles,
And some had ribbonds red as blood,
   All wound about their middles.

The troopers, too, would gallop up
   And fire right in our faces;
It scared me almost half to death
   To see them run such races.

Old uncle Sam, come there to change
   Some pancakes and some onions,
For lasses-cakes to carry home
   To give his wife and young ones.

But I can't tell you half I see
   They kept up such a smother;
So I took my hat off—made a bow,
   And scamper'd home to mother.

BENJAMIN FRANKLIN

2.   *Paper*

(1706–1790)

SOME wit of old—such wits of old there were—
   Whose hints show'd meaning, whose allusions care,
By one brave stroke to mark all human kind,
Call'd clear blank paper every infant mind;
Where still, as opening sense her dictates wrote,
Fair virtue put a seal, or vice a blot.

The thought was happy, pertinent, and true;
Methinks a genius might the plan pursue.
I (can you pardon my presumption?) I—
No wit, no genius, yet for once will try.

12

BENJAMIN FRANKLIN

Various the papers various wants produce,
The wants of fashion, elegance, and use.
Men are as various; and if right I scan,
Each sort of *paper* represents some *man*.

Pray note the fop—half powder and half lace—
Nice as a band-box were his dwelling place:
He's the *gilt paper*, which apart you store,
And lock from vulgar hands in the 'scrutoire.

Mechanics, servants, farmers, and so forth,
Are *copy-paper*, of inferior worth;
Less prized, more useful, for your desk decreed,
Free to all pens, and prompt at every need.

* * * *

The retail politician's anxious thought
Deems *this* side always right, and *that* stark naught;
He foams with censure; with applause he raves—
A dupe to rumors, and a tool of knaves;
He'll want no type his weakness to proclaim,
While such a thing as *foolscap* has a name.

* * * *

What are our poets, take them as they fall,
Good, bad, rich, poor, much read, not read at all?
Them and their works in the same class you'll find;
They are the mere *waste-paper* of mankind.

Observe the maiden, innocently sweet,
She's fair *white-paper*, an unsullied sheet;
On which the happy man, whom fate ordains,
May write his *name*, and take her for his pains.

One instance more, and only one I'll bring;
'T is the *great man* who scorns a little thing,
Whose thoughts, whose deeds, whose maxims are his own,
Form'd on the feelings of his heart alone:
True genuine *royal paper* is his breast:
Of all the kinds most precious, purest, best.

PHILIP FRENEAU

3. *To a Caty-Did*

(1752–1832)

IN a branch of willow hid
Sings the evening Caty-did:
From the lofty locust bough
Feeding on a drop of dew,
In her suit of green arrayed
Hear her singing in the shade—
Caty-did, Caty-did, Caty-did!

While upon a leaf you tread,
Or repose your little head
On your sheet of shadows laid,
All the day you nothing said:
Half the night your cheery tongue
Revelled out its little song,—
Nothing else but Caty-did.

From your lodging on the leaf
Did you utter joy or grief?
Did you only mean to say,
I have had my summer's day,
And am passing, soon, away
To the grave of Caty-did:
Poor, unhappy Caty-did!

But you would have uttered more
Had you known of nature's power;
From the world when you retreat,
And a leaf's your winding sheet,
Long before your spirit fled,
Who can tell but nature said,—
Live again, my Caty-did!
Live, and chatter Caty-did.

14

PHILIP FRENEAU

Tell me what did Caty do?
Did she mean to trouble you?
Why was Caty not forbid
To trouble little Caty-did?
Wrong, indeed, at you to fling,
Hurting no one while you sing,—
Caty-did! Caty-did! Caty-did!

Why continue to complain?
Caty tells me she again
Will not give you plague or pain;
Caty says you may be hid,
Caty will not go to bed
While you sing us Caty-did,—
Caty-did! Caty-did! Caty-did!

But, while singing, you forgot
To tell us what did Caty *not:*
Caty did not think of cold,
Flocks retiring to the fold,
Winter with his wrinkles old;
Winter, that yourself foretold
When you gave us Caty-did.

Stay serenely on your nest;
Caty now will do her best,
All she can, to make you blest;
But you want no human aid,—
Nature, when she formed you, said,
"Independent you are made,
My dear little Caty-did:
Soon yourself must disappear
With the verdure of the year,"
And to go, we know not where,
With your song of Caty-did.

PHILIP FRENEAU

4.
The Parting Glass

THE man that joins in life's career
And hopes to find some comfort here,
To rise above this earthly mass,—
The only way's to drink his glass.

But still, on this uncertain stage
Where hopes and fears the soul engage,
And while, amid the joyous band,
Unheeded flows the measured sand,
Forget not as the moments pass
That time shall bring the parting glass!

The nymph who boasts no borrowed charms,
Whose sprightly wit my fancy warms,—
What though she tends this country inn,
And mixes wine, and deals out gin?
With such a kind, obliging lass,
I sigh to take the parting glass.

With him who always talks of gain
(Dull Momus, of the plodding train),
The wretch who thrives by others' woes,
And carries grief where'er he goes,—
With people of this knavish class
The first is still my parting glass.

With those that drink before they dine,
With him that apes the grunting swine,
Who fills his page with low abuse,
And strives to act the gabbling goose
Turned out by fate to feed on grass—
Boy, give me quick, the parting glass.

PHILIP FRENEAU

The man whose friendship is sincere,
Who knows no guilt, and feels no fear,—
It would require a heart of brass
With him to take the parting glass.

With him who quaffs his pot of ale,
Who holds to all an even scale,
Who hates a knave in each disguise,
And fears him not—whate'er his size—
With him, well pleased my days to pass,
May heaven forbid the Parting Glass!

ST. JOHN HONEYWOOD

5.   *Darby and Joan*

(1763-1798)

I

WHEN Darby saw the setting sun,
    He swung his scythe, and home he run,
Sat down, drank off his quart, and said,
"My work is done, I'll go to bed."
"My work is done!" retorted Joan,
"My work is done! your constant tone;
But hapless woman ne'er can say,
'My work is done,' till judgment day.
You men can sleep all night, but we
Must toil."—"Whose fault is that?" quoth he.
"I know your meaning," Joan replied,
"But, Sir, my tongue shall not be tied;
I will go on, and let you know
What work poor women have to do:
First, in the morning, though we feel
As sick as drunkards when they reel,—
Yee, feel such pains in back and head
As would confine you men to bed,

ST. JOHN HONEYWOOD

We ply the brush, we wield the broom,
We air the beds, and right the room;
The cows must next be milked—and then
We get the breakfast for the men.
Ere this is done, with whimpering cries,
And bristly hair, the children rise;
These must be dressed, and dosed with rue,
And fed—and all because of you:
We next"—Here Darby scratched his head,
And stole off grumbling to his bed;
And only said, as on she run,
"Zounds! woman's clack is never done."

II

At early dawn, ere Phœbus rose,
Old Joan resumed her tale of woes;
When Darby thus—"I'll end the strife,
Be you the man and I the wife:
Take you the scythe and mow, while I
Will all your boasted cares supply."
"Content," quoth Joan, "give me my stint."
This Darby did, and out she went.
Old Darby rose and seized the broom
And whirled the dirt about the room:
Which having done, he scarce knew how,
He hied to milk the brindled cow.
The brindled cow whisked round her tail
In Darby's eyes, and kicked the pail.
The clown, perplexed with grief and pain,
Swore he'd ne'er try to milk again:
When turning round, in sad amaze,
He saw his cottage in a blaze:
For as he chanced to brush the room,
In careless haste, he fired the broom.

ST. JOHN HONEYWOOD

The fire at last subdued, he swore
The broom and he would meet no more.
Pressed by misfortune, and perplext,
Darby prepared for breakfast next;
But what to get he scarcely knew—
The bread was spent, the butter too.
His hands bedaubed with paste and flour,
Old Darby labored full an hour:
But, luckless wight! thou couldst not make
The bread take form of loaf or cake.
As every door wide open stood,
In pushed the sow in quest of food;
And, stumbling onwards, with her snout
O'erset the churn—the cream ran out.
As Darby turned the sow to beat,
The slippery cream betrayed his feet;
He caught the bread trough in his fall,
And down came Darby, trough, and all.
The children, wakened by the clatter,
Start up, and cry, "Oh! what's the matter?"
Old Jowler barked, and Tabby mewed,
And hapless Darby bawled aloud,
"Return, my Joan, as heretofore,
I'll play the housewife's part no more:
Since now, by sad experience taught,
Compared to thine my work is naught;
Henceforth, as business calls, I'll take,
Content, the plough, the scythe, the rake,
And never more transgress the line
Our fates have marked, while thou art mine.
Then Joan, return, as heretofore,
I'll vex thy honest soul no more;
Let's each our proper task attend—
Forgive the past, and strive to mend."

JOHN QUINCY ADAMS

6.
To Sally

(1767–1848)

THE man in righteousness arrayed,
   A pure and blameless liver,
Needs not the keen Toledo blade,
   Nor venom-freighted quiver.
What though he wind his toilsome way
   O'er regions wild and weary—
Through Zara's burning desert stray,
   Or Asia's jungles dreary:

What though he plough the billowy deep
   By lunar light, or solar,
Meet the resistless Simoon's sweep,
   Or iceberg circumpolar!
In bog or quagmire deep and dank
   His foot shall never settle;
He mounts the summit of Mont Blanc,
   Or Popocatapetl.

On Chimborazo's breathless height
   He treads o'er burning lava;
Or snuffs the Bohan Upas blight,
   The deathful plant of Java.
Through every peril he shall pass,
   By Virtue's shield protected;
And still by Truth's unerring glass
   His path shall be directed.

Else wherefore was it, Thursday last,
   While strolling down the valley,
Defenceless, musing as I passed
   A canzonet to Sally,
A wolf, with mouth-protruding snout,
   Forth from the thicket bounded—
I clapped my hands and raised a shout—
   He heard—and fled—confounded.

JOHN QUINCY ADAMS

Tangier nor Tunis never bred
  An animal more crabbed;
Nor Fez, dry-nurse of lions, fed
  A monster half so rabid;
Nor Ararat so fierce a beast
  Has seen since days of Noah;
Nor stronger, eager for a feast,
  The fell constrictor boa.

Oh! place me where the solar beam
  Has scorched all verdure vernal;
Or on the polar verge extreme,
  Blocked up with ice eternal—
Still shall my voice's tender lays
  Of love remain unbroken;
And still my charming Sally praise,
  Sweet smiling and sweet spoken.

7.   *The Lip and the Heart*

ONE day between the Lip and the Heart
    A wordless strife arose,
Which was expertest in the art
  His purpose to disclose.

The Lip called forth the vassal Tongue,
  And made him vouch—a lie!
The slave his servile anthem sung,
  And braved the listening sky.

The Heart to speak in vain essayed,
  Nor could his purpose reach—
His will nor voice nor tongue obeyed,
  His silence was his speech.

JOHN QUINCY ADAMS

Mark thou their difference, child of earth!
    While each performs his part,
Not all the lip can speak is worth
    The silence of the heart.

CLEMENT CLARKE MOORE

8.   *A Visit from St. Nicholas*
                                    (1779–1863)

'TWAS the night before Christmas, when all through
        the house
Not a creature was stirring, not even a mouse;
The stockings were hung by the chimney with care,
In hopes that St. Nicholas soon would be there;
The children were nestled all snug in their beds,
While visions of sugar-plums danced in their heads;
And mamma in her 'kerchief, and I in my cap,
Had just settled our brains for a long winter's nap,
When out on the lawn there arose such a clatter,
I sprang from the bed to see what was the matter.
Away to the window I flew like a flash,
Tore open the shutters and threw up the sash.
The moon on the breast of the new-fallen snow
Gave the lustre of mid-day to objects below,
When, what to my wondering eyes should appear,
But a miniature sleigh, and eight tiny reindeer,
With a little old driver, so lively and quick,
I knew in a moment it must be St. Nick.
More rapid than eagles his coursers they came,
And he whistled, and shouted, and called them by
        name:
"Now, *Dasher!* now, *Dancer!* now, *Prancer* and *Vixen!*
On, *Comet!* on, *Cupid!* on, *Donder* and *Blitzen!*

CLEMENT CLARKE MOORE

To the top of the porch! to the top of the wall!
Now dash away! dash away! dash away all!"
As dry leaves that before the wild hurricane fly,
When they meet with an obstacle, mount to the sky;
So up to the house-top the coursers they flew,
With the sleigh full of Toys, and St. Nicholas too.
And then, in a twinkling, I heard on the roof
The prancing and pawing of each little hoof.
As I drew in my head, and was turning around,
Down the chimney St. Nicholas came with a bound.
He was dressed all in fur, from his head to his foot,
And his clothes were all tarnished with ashes and soot;
A bundle of Toys he had flung on his back,
And he looked like a pedler just opening his pack.
His eyes—how they twinkled! his dimples how merry!
His cheeks were like roses, his nose like a cherry!
His droll little mouth was drawn up like a bow,
And the beard of his chin was as white as the snow;
The stump of a pipe he held tight in his teeth,
And the smoke it encircled his head like a wreath;
He had a broad face and a little round belly,
That shook when he laughed, like a bowlful of jelly.
He was chubby and plump, a right jolly old elf,
And I laughed when I saw him, in spite of myself;
A wink of his eye and a twist of his head,
Soon gave me to know I had nothing to dread;
He spoke not a word, but went straight to his work,
And filled all the stockings; then turned with a jerk,
And laying his finger aside of his nose,
And giving a nod, up the chimney he rose;
He sprang to his sleigh, to his team gave a whistle,
And away they all flew like the down of a thistle.
But I heard him exclaim, ere he drove out of sight,
"Happy Christmas to all, and to all a good-night."

23

JOSEPH SMITH

9. *Eulogium on Rum*

* * * *

HAIL, Mighty Rum! how wondrous is thy pow'r!
  Unwarmed by thee how would our spirits fail,
When dark December comes, with aspect sour,
  And, sharp as razor, blows the northern gale!
And yet thou'rt grateful in that sultry day
When raging Sirius darts his fervid ray.

* * * *

But lo! th' ingratitude of Adam's race—
  Though all these clever things to Rum we owe—
Gallons of ink are squirted in his face;
  And his bruis'd back is bang'd with many a blow;
Some hounds of note have sung his funeral knell,
And ev'ry puppy joins the gen'ral yell.

* * * *

But fear not, Rum, tho' fiercely they assail,
  And none but I, the bard, thy cause defend,
Think not thy foes—tho' num'rous—shall prevail,
  Thy pow'r diminish, or thy being end:
Tho' spurned from table, and the public eye,
In the snug closet safely shalt thou lie.

And oft, when Sol's proud chariot quits the sky
  And humbler Cynthia mounts her one-horse chair,
To that snug closet shall thy vot'ry fly;
  And, wrapt in darkness, keep his orgies there;
Lift the full bottle joyous to his head,
Then, great as Caesar, reel sublime to bed.

Burlington, N. J.
December 7, 1789

RALPH WALDO EMERSON

10.   *The Humble-Bee*

(1803-1882)

BURLY, dozing humble-bee,
    Where thou art is clime for me.
Let them sail for Porto Rique,
Far-off heats through seas to seek;
I will follow thee alone,
Thou animated torrid-zone!
Zigzag steerer, desert cheerer,
Let me chase thy waving lines;
Keep me nearer, me thy hearer,
Singing over shrubs and vines.

Insect lover of the sun,
Joy of thy dominion!
Sailor of the atmosphere;
Swimmer through the waves of air;
Voyager of light and noon;
Epicurean of June;
Wait, I prithee, till I come
Within earshot of thy hum,—
All without is martyrdom.

When the south wind, in May days,
With a net of shining haze
Silvers the horizon wall,
And with softness touching all,
Tints the human countenance
With the color of romance,
And infusing subtle heats,
Turns the sod to violets,
Thou, in sunny solitudes,
Rover of the underwoods,
The green silence dost displace
With thy mellow, breezy bass.

RALPH WALDO EMERSON

Hot midsummer's petted crone,
Sweet to me thy drowsy tone
Tells of countless sunny hours,
Long days, and solid banks of flowers;
Of gulfs of sweetness without bound
In Indian wildernesses found;
Of Syrian peace, immortal leisure,
Firmest cheer, and bird-like pleasure.

Aught unsavory or unclean
Hath my insect never seen;
But violets and bilberry bells,
Maple-sap and daffodels,
Grass with green flag half-mast high,
Succory to match the sky,
Columbine with horn of honey,
Scented fern and agrimony,
Clover, catchfly, adder's-tongue
And brier-roses, dwelt among;
All beside was unknown waste,
All was picture as he passed.

Wiser far than human seer,
Yellow-breeched philosopher
Seeing only what is fair,
Sipping only what is sweet,
Thou dost mock at fate and care,
Leave the chaff and take the wheat.
When the fierce northwestern blast
Cools sea and land so far and fast,
Thou already slumberest deep;
Woe and want thou canst outsleep;
Want and woe, which torture us,
Thy sleep makes ridiculous.

NATHANIEL PARKER WILLIS

11.   *Love in a Cottage*

(1806-1867)

THEY may talk of love in a cottage,
   And bowers of trelised vine—
Of nature bewitchingly simple,
   And milkmaids half divine;
They may talk of the pleasures of sleeping
   In the shade of a spreading tree,
And a walk in the fields at morning,
   By the side of a footstep free!

But give me a sly flirtation
   By the light of a chandelier—
With music to play in the pauses,
   And nobody very near;
Or a seat on a silken sofa,
   With a glass of pure old wine,
And mamma too blind to discover
   The small white hand in mine.

Your love in a cottage is hungry,
   Your vine is a nest for flies—
Your milkmaid shocks the Graces,
   And simplicity talks of pies!
You lie down to your shady slumber
   And wake with a bug in your ear,
And your damsel that walks in the morning
   Is shod like a mountaineer.

True love is at home on a carpet,
   And mightily likes his ease—
And true love has an eye for a dinner,
   And starves beneath shady trees.

NATHANIEL PARKER WILLIS

His wing is the fan of a lady,
 His foot's an invisible thing,
And his arrow is tipp'd with a jewel
 And shot from a silver string.

CHARLES FENNO HOFFMAN

12.   *"Sparkling and Bright"*

(1806–1884)

SPARKLING and bright in liquid light,
 Does the wine our goblets gleam in;
With hue as red as the rosy bed
 Which a bee would choose to dream in.
 Then fill to-night, with hearts as light,
  To loves as gay and fleeting
 As bubbles that swim on the beaker's brim,
  And break on the lips while meeting.

Oh! if Mirth might arrest the flight
 Of Time through Life's dominions,
We here a while would now beguile
 The graybeard of his pinions,
 To drink to-night, with hearts as light,
  To loves as gay and fleeting
 As bubbles that swim on the beaker's brim,
  And break on the lips while meeting.

But since Delight can't tempt the wight,
 Nor fond Regret delay him,
Nor Love himself can hold the elf,
 Nor sober Friendship stay him,
 We'll drink to-night, with hearts as light,
  To loves as gay and fleeting
 As bubbles that swim on the beaker's brim,
  And break on the lips while meeting.

HENRY WADSWORTH LONGFELLOW

13.   *Catawba Wine*

(1807–1882)

THIS song of mine
  Is a Song of the Vine,
To be sung by the glowing embers
  Of wayside inns,
  When the rain begins
To darken the drear Novembers.

  It is not a song
  Of the Scuppernong,
From warm Carolinian valleys,
  Nor the Isabel
  And the Muscadel
That bask in our garden alleys.

  Nor the red Mustang,
  Whose clusters hang
O'er the waves of the Colorado,
  And the fiery flood
  Of whose purple blood
Has a dash of Spanish bravado.

  For richest and best
  Is the wine of the West,
That grows by the Beautiful River;
  Whose sweet perfume
  Fills all the room
With a benison on the giver.

  And as hollow trees
  Are the haunts of bees,
Forever going and coming;
  So this crystal hive
  Is all alive
With a swarming and buzzing and humming.

HENRY WADSWORTH LONGFELLOW

Very good in its way
Is the Verzenay,
Or the Sillery soft and creamy;
But Catawba wine
Has a taste more divine,
More dulcet, delicious, and dreamy.

There grows no vine
By the haunted Rhine,
By Danube or Guadalquiver,
Nor on island or cape,
That bears such a grape
As grows by the Beautiful River.

Drugged in their juice
For foreign use,
When shipped o'er the reeling Atlantic,
To rack our brains
With the fever pains,
That have driven the Old World frantic.

To the sewers and sinks
With all such drinks,
And after them tumble the mixer;
For a poison malign
Is such Borgia's wine,
Or at best but a Devil's Elixir.

While pure as a spring
Is the wine I sing,
And to praise it, one needs but name it;
For Catawba wine
Has need of no sign,
No tavern-bush to proclaim it.

HENRY WADSWORTH LONGFELLOW

And this Song of the Vine,
This greeting of mine,
The winds and the birds shall deliver
To the Queen of the West,
In her garlands dressed,
On the banks of the Beautiful River.

OLIVER WENDELL HOLMES

14.   *The Last Leaf*

(1809-1894)

I SAW him once before,
   As he passed by the door,
       And again
The pavement stones resound,
As he totters o'er the ground
       With his cane.

They say that in his prime,
Ere the pruning-knife of Time
       Cut him down,
Not a better man was found
By the Crier on his round
       Through the town.

But now he walks the streets,
And he looks at all he meets
       Sad and wan,
And he shakes his feeble head,
That it seems as if he said,
       "They are gone."

31

OLIVER WENDELL HOLMES

The mossy marbles rest
On the lips that he has pressed
   In their bloom,
And the names he loved to hear
Have been carved for many a year
   On the tomb.

My grandmamma has said,—
Poor old lady, she is dead
   Long ago,—
That he had a Roman nose,
And his cheek was like a rose
   In the snow:

But now his nose is thin,
And it rests upon his chin
   Like a staff,
And a crook is in his back,
And a melancholy crack
   In his laugh.

I know it is a sin
For me to sit and grin
   At him here;
But the old three-cornered hat,
And the breeches, and all that,
   Are so queer!

And if I should live to be
The last leaf upon the tree
   In the spring,
Let them smile, as I do now,
At the old forsaken bough
   Where I cling.

OLIVER WENDELL HOLMES

15. *The Height of the Ridiculous*

I WROTE some lines once on a time
   In wondrous merry mood,
And thought, as usual, men would say
   They were exceeding good.

They were so queer, so very queer,
   I laughed as I would die;
Albeit, in the general way,
   A sober man am I.

I called my servant, and he came;
   How kind it was of him,
To mind a slender man like me,
   He of the mighty limb!

"These to the printer," I exclaimed,
   And, in my humorous way,
I added (as a trifling jest),
   "There'll be the devil to pay."

He took the paper, and I watched,
   And saw him peep within;
At the first line he read, his face
   Was all upon the grin.

He read the next; the grin grew broad,
   And shot from ear to ear;
He read the third; a chuckling noise
   I now began to hear.

The fourth; he broke into a roar;
   The fifth; his waistband split;
The sixth; he burst five buttons off,
   And tumbled in a fit.

Ten days and nights, with sleepless eye,
I watched that wretched man,
And since, I never dare to write
As funny as I can.

16. *The Deacon's Masterpiece, or the Wonderful "One-Hoss Shay"*

A LOGICAL STORY

HAVE you heard of the wonderful one-hoss shay,
That was built in such a logical way
It ran a hundred years to a day,
And then, of a sudden, it—ah, but stay,
I'll tell you what happened without delay,
Scaring the parson into fits,
Frightening people out of their wits,—
Have you ever heard of that, I say?

Seventeen hundred and fifty-five.
Georgius Secundus was then alive,—
Snuffy old drone from the German hive.
That was the year when Lisbon-town
Saw the earth open and gulp her down,
And Braddock's army was done so brown,
Left without a scalp to its crown.
It was on the terrible Earthquake-day
That the Deacon finished the one-hoss shay.

Now in building of chaises, I tell you what,
There is always *somewhere* a weakest spot,—
In hub, tire, felloe, in spring or thill,
In panel, or crossbar, or floor, or sill,
In screw, bolt, thoroughbrace,—lurking still,
Find it somewhere you must and will,—

34

OLIVER WENDELL HOLMES

Above or below, or within or without,—
And that's the reason, beyond a doubt,
That a chaise *breaks down*, but doesn't *wear out*.

But the Deacon swore (as Deacons do,
With an "I dew vum," or an "I tell *yeou*,")
He would build one shay to beat the taown
'N' the keounty 'n' all the kentry raoun';
It should be so built that it *couldn'* break daown:
"Fur," said the Deacon, "'t's mighty plain
Thut the weakes' place mus' stan' the strain;
'N' the way t' fix it, uz I maintain,
                    Is only jest
T' make that place uz strong uz the rest."

So the Deacon inquired of the village folk
Where he could find the strongest oak,
That couldn't be split nor bent nor broke,—
That was for spokes and floor and sills;
He sent for lancewood to make the thills;
The crossbars were ash, from the straightest trees,
The panels of white-wood, that cuts like cheese,
But lasts like iron for things like these;
The hubs of logs from the "Settler's ellum,"—
Last of its timber,—they couldn't sell 'em,
Never an axe had seen their chips,
And the wedges flew from between their lips,
Their blunt ends frizzled like celery-tips;
Step and prop-iron, bolt and screw,
Spring, tire, axle, and linchpin too,
Steel of the finest, bright and blue;
Thoroughbrace bison-skin, thick and wide;
Boot, top, dasher, from tough old hide
Found in the pit when the tanner died.
That was the way he "put her through."
"There!" said the Deacon, "naow she'll dew!"

OLIVER WENDELL HOLMES

Do! I tell you, I rather guess
She was a wonder, and nothing less!
Colts grew horses, beards turned gray,
Deacon and deaconess dropped away,
Children and grandchildren—where were they?
But there stood the stout old one-hoss shay
As fresh as on Lisbon-earthquake-day!

EIGHTEEN HUNDRED;—it came and found
The Deacon's masterpiece strong and sound.
Eighteen hundred increased by ten;
"Hahnsum kerridge" they called it then.
Eighteen hundred and twenty came;—
Running as usual; much the same.
Thirty and Forty at last arrive,
And then come Fifty, and FIFTY-FIVE.

Little of all we value here
Wakes on the morn of its hundredth year
Without both feeling and looking queer.
In fact, there's nothing that keeps its youth,
So far as I know, but a tree and truth.
(This is a moral that runs at large;
Take it.—You're welcome.—No extra charge.)

FIRST OF NOVEMBER,—the Earthquake-day,—
There are traces of age in the one-hoss shay.
A general flavor of mild decay,
But nothing local, as one may say.
There couldn't be,—for the Deacon's art
Had made it so like in every part
That there wasn't a chance for one to start.
For the wheels were just as strong as the thills,
And the floor was just as strong as the sills,
And the panels just as strong as the floor,
36

OLIVER WENDELL HOLMES

And the whipple-tree neither less nor more,
And the back-crossbar as strong as the fore,
And spring and axle and hub *encore*.
And yet, *as a whole*, it is past a doubt
In another hour it will be *worn out!*

First of November, Fifty-five!
This morning the parson takes a drive.
Now, small boys, get out of the way!
Here comes the wonderful one-hoss shay,
Drawn by a rat-railed, ewe-necked bay.
"Huddup!" said the parson.—Off went they.

The parson was working his Sunday's text,—
Had got to *fifthly*, and stopped perplexed
At what the—Moses—was coming next.
All at once the horse stood still,
Close by the meet'n'-house on the hill.
First a shiver, and then a thrill,
Then something decidedly like a spill,—
And the parson was sitting upon a rock,
At half past nine by the meet'n'-house clock,—
Just the hour of the Earthquake shock!
What do you think the parson found,
When he got up and stared around?
The poor old chaise in a heap or mound,
As if it had been to the mill and ground!
You see, of course, if you're not a dunce,
How it went to pieces all at once,—
All at once, and nothing first,—
Just as bubbles do when they burst.

End of the wonderful one-hoss shay.
Logic is logic. That's all I say.

JAMES THOMAS FIELDS

The Alarmed Skipper

(1816–1881)

MANY a long, long year ago,
  Nantucket skippers had a plan
Of finding out, though "lying low,"
  How near New York their schooners ran.

They greased the lead before it fell,
  And then by sounding, through the night,
Knowing the soil that stuck so well,
  They always guessed their reckoning right.

A skipper gray, whose eyes were dim,
  Could tell, by tasting, just the spot;
And so below he'd "douse the glim,"—
  After, of course, his "something hot."

Snug in his berth, at eight o'clock,
  This ancient skipper might be found;
No matter how his craft would rock,
  He slept,—for skippers' naps are sound.

The watch on deck would now and then
  Run down and wake him, with the lead;
He'd up and taste, and tell the men
  How many miles they went ahead.

One night 'twas Jotham Marden's watch,
  A curious wag—the peddler's son;
And so he mused (the wanton wretch!)
  "To-night I'll have a grain of fun.

"We're all a set of stupid fools,
  To think the skipper knows, by tasting,
What ground he's on; Nantucket schools
  Don't teach such stuff, with all their basting!"

38

JAMES THOMAS FIELDS

And so he took the well-greased lead,
   And rubbed it o'er a box of earth
That stood on deck—a parsnip-bed,—
   And then he sought the skipper's berth.

"Where are we now, sir?   Please to taste."
   The skipper yawned, put out his tongue,
Opened his eyes in wondrous haste,
   And then upon the floor he sprung.

The skipper stormed, and tore his hair,
   Hauled on his boots, and roared to Marden,
"Nantucket's sunk, and here we are
   Right over old Marm Hackett's garden!"

JOHN GODFREY SAXE

18.　　　*The Mourner à la Mode*

(1816–1887)

I SAW her last night at a party
   (The elegant party at Mead's),
And looking remarkably hearty
   For a widow so young in her weeds;
Yet I know she was suffering sorrow
   Too deep for the tongue to express,—
Or why had she chosen to borrow
   So much from the language of dress?

Her shawl was as sable as night;
   And her gloves were as dark as her shawl;
And her jewels—that flashed in the light—
   Were black as a funeral pall;
Her robe had the hue of the rest,
   (How nicely it fitted her shape!)
And the grief that was heaving her breast
   Boiled over in billows of crape!

JOHN GODFREY SAXE

What tears of vicarious woe,
   That else might have sullied her face,
Were kindly permitted to flow
   In ripples of ebony lace!
While even her fan, in its play,
   Had quite a lugubrious scope,
And seemed to be waving away
   The ghost of the angel of Hope!

Yet rich as the robes of a queen
   Was the sombre apparel she wore;
I'm certain I never had seen
   Such a sumptuous sorrow before;
And I couldn't help thinking the beauty,
   In mourning the loved and the lost,
Was doing her conjugal duty
   Altogether regardless of cost!

One surely would say a devotion
   Performed at so vast an expense
Betrayed an excess of emotion
   That was really something immense;
And yet as I viewed, at my leisure,
   Those tokens of tender regard,
I thought:—It is scarce without measure—
   The sorrow that goes by the yard!

Ah! grief is a curious passion;
   And yours—I am sorely afraid
The very next phase of the fashion
   Will find it beginning to fade;
Though dark are the shadows of grief,
   The morning will follow the night,
Half-tints will betoken relief,
   Till joy shall be symboled in white!

JOHN GODFREY SAXE

Ah well! it were idle to quarrel
    With Fashion, or aught she may do;
And so I conclude with a moral
    And metaphor—warranted new:—
When *measles* come handsomely out,
    The patient is safest, they say;
And the *Sorrow* is mildest, no doubt,
    That works in a similar way!

JAMES RUSSELL LOWELL

19.   *The Courtin'*

(1819–1891)

GOD makes sech nights, all white an' still
    Fur 'z you can look or listen,
Moonshine an' snow on field an' hill,
    All silence an' all glisten.

Zekle crep' up quite unbeknown
    An' peeked in thru' the winder,
An' there sot Huldy all alone,
    'ith no one nigh to hender.

A fireplace filled the room's one side,
    With half a cord o' wood in—
There warn't no stoves (tell comfort died)
    To bake ye to a puddin'.

The wa'nut logs shot sparkles out
    Towards the pootiest, bless her!
An' leetle flames danced all about
    The chiny on the dresser.

Agin the chimbley crook-necks hung,
    An' in amongst 'em rusted
The ole queen's arm thet gran'ther Young
    Fetched back f'om Concord busted.

41

JAMES RUSSELL LOWELL

The very room, coz she was in,
    Seemed warm f'om floor to ceilin',
An' she looked full ez rosy agin
    Ez the apples she was peelin'.

'Twas kin' o' kingdom-come to look
    On sech a blessèd cretur,
A dogrose blushin' to a brook
    Ain't modester nor sweeter.

He was six foot o' man, A 1,
    Clear grit an' human natur';
None couldn't quicker pitch a ton,
    Nor dror a furrer straighter.

He'd sparked it with full twenty gals,
    He'd squired 'em, danced 'em, druv 'em,
Fust this one, an' then thet, by spells—
    All is, he couldn't love 'em.

But long o' her his veins 'ould run
    All crinkly like curled maple,
The side she breshed felt full o' sun
    Ez a south slope in Ap'il.

She thought no v'ice hed sech a swing
    Ez hisn in the choir;
My! when he made Ole Hundred ring,
    She *knowed* the Lord was nigher.

An' she'd blush scarlit, right in prayer,
    When her new meetin'-bunnet
Felt somehow thru' its crown a pair
    O' blue eyes sot upun it.

JAMES RUSSELL LOWELL

Thet night, I tell ye, she looked *some!*
  She seemed to've gut a new soul,
For she felt sartin-sure he'd come,
  Down to her very shoe-sole.

She heered a foot, an' knowed it tu,
  A-raspin' on the scraper,—
All ways to once her feelin's flew
  Like sparks in burnt-up paper.

He kin' o' l'itered on the mat,
  Some doubtfle o' the sekle,
His heart kep' goin' pitty-pat,
  But hern went pity Zekle.

An' yit she gin her cheer a jerk
  Ez though she wished him furder,
An' on her apples kep' to work,
  Parin' away like murder.

"You want to see my Pa, I s'pose?"
  "Wal . . . no . . . I come dasignin' "—
"To see my Ma? She's sprinklin' clo'es
  Agin to-morrer's i'nin'."

To say why gals acts so or so,
  Or don't, 'ould be presumin';
Mebby to mean *yes* an' say *no*
  Comes nateral to women.

He stood a spell on one foot fust,
  Then stood a spell on t'other,
An' on which one he felt the wust
  He couldn't ha' told ye nuther.

Says he, "I'd better call ag'in";
  Says she, "Think likely, Mister";
Thet last word pricked him like a pin,
  An' . . . Wal, he up an' kissed her.

When Ma bimeby upon 'em slips,
  Huldy sot pale ez ashes,
All kin' o' smily roun' the lips
  An' teary roun' the lashes.

For she was jes' the quiet kind
  Whose naturs never vary,
Like streams that keep a summer mind
  Snow-hid in Jenooary.

The blood clost roun' her heart felt glued
  Too tight for all expressin',
Tell mother see how metters stood
  And gin 'em both her blessin'.

Then her red come back like the tide
  Down to the Bay o' Fundy,
An' all I know is they was cried
  In meetin' come nex' Sunday.

20.   *What Mr. Robinson Thinks*

GUVENER B. is a sensible man;
    He stays to his home an' looks arter his folks;
He draws his furrer ez straight ez he can,
  An' into nobody's tater-patch pokes;
        But John P.
        Robinson he
    Sez he wunt vote fer Guvener B.

JAMES RUSSELL LOWELL

My! aint it terrible?   Wut shall we du?
  We can't never choose him o' course,—thet's flat;
Guess we shall hev to come round, (don't you?)
  An' go in fer thunder an' guns, an' all that;
      Fer John P.
      Robinson he
  Sez he wunt vote fer Guvener B.

Gineral C. is a dreffle smart man:
  He's ben on all sides that give places or pelf;
But consistency still wuz a part of his plan,—
  He's ben true to *one* party,—an' thet is himself;—
      So John P.
      Robinson he
  Sez he shall vote fer Gineral C.

Gineral C. he goes in fer the war;
  He don't vally princerple more'n an old cud;
Wut did God make us raytional creeturs fer,
  But glory an' gunpowder, plunder an' blood?
      So John P.
      Robinson he
  Sez he shall vote fer Gineral C.

We were gittin' on nicely up here to our village,
  With good old idees o' wut's right an' wut aint,
We kind o' thought Christ went agin war an' pillage,
  An' thet eppyletts worn't the best mark of a saint;
      But John P.
      Robinson he
  Sez this kind o' thing's an exploded idee.

The side of our country must ollers be took,
  An' Presidunt Polk, you know, *he* is our country,
An' the angel thet writes all our sins in a book
  Puts the *debit* to him, an' to us the *per contry;*

JAMES RUSSELL LOWELL

An' John P.
Robinson he
Sez this is his view o' the thing to a T.

Parson Wilbur he calls all these argimunts lies;
   Sez they're nothin' on airth but jest *fee, faw, fum*;
An' thet all this big talk of our destinies
   Is half on it ign'ance, an' t'other half rum;
      But John P.
      Robinson he
   Sez it aint no sech thing; an', of course, so must we.

Parson Wilbur sez *he* never heerd in his life
   That th' Apostles rigged out in their swaller-tail coats,
An' marched round in front of a drum an' a fife,
   To git some on 'em office, an' some on 'em votes;
      But John P.
      Robinson he
   Sez they didn't know everythin' down in Judee.

Wal, it's a marcy we've gut folks to tell us
   The rights an' the wrongs o' these matters, I vow,—
God sends country lawyers, an' other wise fellers,
   To start the world's team wen it gits in a slough;
      Fer John P.
      Robinson he
   Sez the world'll go right, ef he hollers out Gee!

CHARLES GODFREY LELAND

21.   *Hans Breitmann's Party*

(1824–1903)

H ANS BREITMANN gife a barty,
      Dey had biano-blayin;
I felled in lofe mit a Merican frau,
   Her name was Madilda Yane.

46

CHARLES GODFREY LELAND

She hat haar as prown ash a pretzel,
  Her eyes vas himmel-plue,
Und ven dey looket indo mine,
  Dey shplit mine heart in two.

Hans Breitmann gife a barty,
  I vent dere you'll pe pound.
I valset mit Madilda Yane
  Und vent shpinnen round und round.
De pootiest Frauelein in de House,
  She vayed 'pout dwo hoondred pound,
Und efery dime she give a shoomp
  She make de vindows sound.

Hans Breitmann gife a barty,
  I dells you it cost him dear.
Dey rolled in more ash sefen kecks
  Of foost-rate Lager Beer.
Und venefer dey knocks de shpicket in
  De Deutschers gifes a cheer.
I dinks dat so vine a barty
  Nefer coom to a het dis year.

Hans Breitmann gife a barty;
  Dere all vas Souse und Brouse,
Ven de sooper coomed in, de gompany
  Did make demselfs to house;
Dey ate das Brot und Gensy broost,
  De Bratwurst und Braten fine,
Und vash der Abendessen down
  Mit four parrels of Neckarwein.

Hans Breitmann gife a barty;
  We all cot troonk ash bigs.
I poot mine mout to a parrel of bier,
  Und emptied it oop mit a schwigs.

CHARLES GODFREY LELAND

Und denn I gissed Madilda Yane
    Und she shlog me on de kop,
Und de gompany fited mit daple-lecks
    Dill de coonshtable made oos shtop.

Hans Breitmann gife a barty—
    Where ish dat barty now?
Where ish de lofely golden cloud
    Dat float on de moundains' prow?
Where ish de himmelstrahlende Stern—
    De shtar of de shpirit's light?
All goned afay mit de Lager Beer—
    Afay in de Ewigkeit!

SILAS WEIR MITCHELL

(1829–1914)

22. *A Decanter of Madeira, Aged 86, to George Bancroft, Aged 86, Greeting*

GOOD Master, you and I were born
    In "Teacup days" of hoop and hood,
And when the silver cue hung down,
    And toasts were drunk, and wine was good;

When kin of mine (a jolly brood)
    From sideboards looked, and knew full well
What courage they had given the beau,
    How generous made the blushing belle.

Ah me! what gossip could I prate
    Of days when doors were locked at dinners!
Believe me, I have kissed the lips
    Of many pretty saints—or sinners.

48

SILAS WEIR MITCHELL

Lip service have I done, alack!
　I don't repent, but come what may,
What ready lips, sir, I have kissed,
　Be sure at least I shall not say.

Two honest gentlemen are we,—
　I Demi John, whole George are you;
When Nature grew us one in years
　She meant to make a generous brew.

She bade me store for festal hours
　The sun our south-side vineyard knew;
To sterner tasks she set your life,
　As statesman, writer, scholar, grew.

Years eight-six have come and gone;
　At last we meet.   Your health to-night.
Take from this board of friendly hearts
　The memory of a proud delight.

The days that went have made you wise,
　There's wisdom in my rare bouquet.
I'm rather paler than I was;
　And, on my soul, you're growing gray.

I like to think, when Toper Time
　Has drained the last of me and you,
Some here shall say, They both were good,—
　The wine we drank, the man we knew.

23. *Autumn*

(1830-1886)

THE morns are meeker than they were,
  The nuts are getting brown;
The berry's cheek is plumper,
The rose is out of town.
The maple wears a gayer scarf,
The field a scarlet gown.
Lest I should be old-fashioned,
I'll put a trinket on.

24. *The Waking Year*

A LADY red upon the hill
  Her annual secret keeps;
A lady white within the field
  In placid lily sleeps!

The tidy breezes with their brooms
  Sweep vale, and hill, and tree!
Prithee, my pretty housewives!
  Who may expected be?

The neighbors do not yet suspect!
  The woods exchange a smile,—
Orchard, and buttercup, and bird,
  In such a little while!

And yet how still the landscape stands,
  How nonchalant the wood,
As if the resurrection
  Were nothing very odd!

EDMUND CLARENCE STEDMAN

25.   *The Doorstep*

(1833-1908)

THE conference-meeting through at last,
　　We boys around the vestry waited
To see the girls come tripping past,
　　Like snow-birds willing to be mated.

Not braver he that leaps the wall
　　By level musket-flashes bitten,
Than I, that stepped before them all
　　Who longed to see me get the mitten.

But no! she blushed and took my arm:
　　We let the old folks have the highway,
And started toward the Maple Farm
　　Along a kind of lovers' by-way.

I can't remember what we said,—
　　'Twas nothing worth a song or story;
Yet that rude path by which we sped
　　Seemed all transformed and in a glory.

The snow was crisp beneath our feet,
　　The moon was full, the fields were gleaming;
By hood and tippet sheltered sweet,
　　Her face with youth and health was beaming.

The little hand outside her muff
　　(O sculptor! if you could but mold it)
So lightly touched my jacket-cuff,
　　To keep it warm I had to hold it.

To have her with me there alone,—
　　'Twas love and fear and triumph blended:
At last we reached the foot-worn stone
　　Where that delicious journey ended.

51

The old folks, too, were almost home:
　Her dimpled hand the latches fingered,
We heard the voices nearer come,
　Yet on the doorstep still we lingered.

She shook her ringlets from her hood,
　And with a "Thank you, Ned!" dissembled;
But yet I knew she understood
　With what a daring wish I trembled.

A cloud passed kindly overhead,
　The moon was slyly peeping through it,
Yet hid its face, as if it said—
　"Come, now or never! do it! *do it!*"

My lips till then had only known
　The kiss of mother and of sister,—
But somehow, full upon her own
　Sweet, rosy, darling mouth,—I kissed her!

Perhaps 'twas boyish love: yet still,
　O listless woman! weary lover!
To feel once more that fresh, wild thrill
　I'd give—but who can live youth over?

CHARLES FREDERICK JOHNSON

26.　　　*The Modern Romans*
　　　　　　　　　　　　　　　(1836-　　)

UNDER the slanting light of the yellow sun of
　　October,
A "Gang of Dagos" were working close by the side of
the car track.

50

CHARLES FREDERICK JOHNSON

Pausing a moment to catch a note of their liquid
    Italian,
Faintly I heard an echo of Rome's imperial accents,
Broken-down forms of Latin words from the Senate and
    Forum
Now smoothed over by use to the musical lingua
    Romana.
Then came the thought, Why, these are the heirs of the
    conquering Romans;
These are the sons of the men who founded the Empire
    of Caesar;
These are they whose fathers carried the conquering
    eagles
Over all Gaul and across the sea to Ultima Thule.
The race-type persists unchanged in their eyes, and
    profiles and figures—
Muscular, short and thick-set, with prominent noses,
    recalling
"Romanos rerum dominos, gentemque togatam."
See, Labienus is swinging a pick with rhythmical
    motion;
Yonder one pushing the shovel might be Julius
    Caesar,
Lean, deep-eyed, broad-browed, and bald, a man of a
    thousand;
Further along stands the jolly Horatius Flaccus;
Grim and grave, with rings in his ears, see Cato the
    Censor;
And the next has precisely the bust of Cneius Pompeius.
Blurred and worn the surface, I grant, and the coin is
    but copper;
Look more closely, you'll catch a hint of the old super-
    scription—
Perhaps the stem of a letter, perhaps a leaf of the
    laurel.

CHARLES FREDERICK JOHNSON

On the side of the street, in proud and gloomy seclusion,
"Bossing the job," stood a Celt, the race enslaved by
the legions,
Sold in the market of Rome, to meet the expenses of
Caesar.
And as I loitered, the Celt cried, " 'Tind to your worruk,
ye Dagos,
Full up yer shovel, Paythro', ye haythen, I'll dock yees
a quarther."
This he said to the one who resembled the great
Imperator;
Meekly the dignified Roman kept on patiently digging.

Such are the changes and chances, the centuries bring
to the nations.
Surely, the ups and downs of this world are past
calculation.
How the races troop o'er the stage in endless procession!
Persian, and Arab, and Greek, and Hun, and Roman,
and Vandal,
Master the world in turn and then disappear in the
darkness,
Leaving a remnant as hewers of wood and drawers of
water.
"Possibly,"—this I thought to myself—"the yoke of
the Irish
May in turn be lifted from us in the tenth genera-
tion.
Now the Celt is on top, but time may bring his
revenges;
Turning the Fenian down once more to be 'bossed by a
Dago.'"

THOMAS BAILEY ALDRICH

27.   *Thalia*
(1837-1907)

A middle-aged Lyrical poet is supposed to be taking
final leave of the Muse of Comedy. She has brought
him his hat and gloves, and is abstractedly picking
a thread of gold hair from his coat sleeve as he
begins to speak:

I SAY it under the rose—
   oh, thanks!—yes, under the laurel,
We part lovers, not foes;
   we are not going to quarrel.

We have too long been friends
   on foot and in gilded coaches,
Now that the whole thing ends,
   to spoil our kiss with reproaches.

I leave you; my soul is wrung;
   I pause, look back from the portal—
Ah, I no more am young,
   and you, child, you are immortal!

Mine is the glacier's way,
   yours is the blossom's weather—
When were December and May
   known to be happy together?

Before my kisses grow tame,
   before my moodiness grieve you,
While yet my heart is flame,
   and I all lover, I leave you.

THOMAS BAILEY ALDRICH

So, in the coming time,
   when you count the rich years over,
Think of me in my prime,
   and not as a white-haired lover,

Fretful, pierced with regret,
   the wraith of a dead Desire
Thrumming a cracked spinet
   by a slowly dying fire.

When, at last, I am cold—
   years hence, if the gods so will it—
Say, "He was true as gold,"
   and wear a rose in your fillet!

Others, tender as I,
   will come and sue for caresses,
Woo you, win you, and die—
   mind you, a rose in your tresses!

Some Melpomene woo,
   some hold Clio the nearest;
You, sweet Comedy—you
   were ever sweetest and dearest!

Nay, it is time to go.
   When writing your tragic sister
Say to that child of woe
   how sorry I was I missed her.

Really, I cannot stay,
   though "parting is such sweet sorrow" . . .
Perhaps I will, on my way
   down-town, look in to-morrow!

THOMAS BAILEY ALDRICH

28. *The World's Way*

AT Haroun's court it chanced, upon a time,
An Arab poet made this pleasant rhyme:

"The new moon is a horseshoe, wrought of God,
Wherewith the Sultan's stallion shall be shod."

On hearing this, the Sultan smiled, and gave
The man a gold-piece. *Sing again, O slave!*

Above his lute the happy singer bent,
And turned another gracious compliment.

And, as before, the smiling Sultan gave
The man a sekkah. *Sing again, O slave!*

Again the verse came, fluent as a rill
That wanders, silver-footed, down a hill.

The Sultan, listening, nodded as before,
Still gave the gold, and still demanded more.

The nimble fancy that had climbed so high
Grew weary with its climbing by and by:

Strange discords rose; the sense went quite amiss;
The singer's rhymes refused to meet and kiss:

Invention flagged, the lute had got unstrung,
And twice he sang the song already sung.

The Sultan, furious, called a mute, and said,
O Musta, straightway whip me off his head!

Poets! not in Arabia alone
You get beheaded when your skill is gone.

THOMAS BAILEY ALDRICH

29.   *"Forever and a Day"*

I LITTLE know or care
  If the blackbird on the bough
Is filling all the air
With his soft crescendo now;
    For she is gone away,
    And when she went she took
    The springtime in her look,
    The peachblow on her cheek,
    The laughter from the brook,
    The blue from out the May—
    And what she calls a week
    Is forever and a day!

It's little that I mind
How the blossoms, pink or white,
At every touch of wind
Fall a-trembling with delight;
    For in the leafy lane,
    Beneath the garden-boughs,
    And through the silent house
    One thing alone I seek.
    Until she come again
    The May is not the May,
    And what she calls a week
    Is forever and a day!

FRANCIS BRET HARTE

30.   *The Aged Stranger*

AN INCIDENT OF THE WAR

(1839–1902)

"I WAS with Grant"—the stranger said;
    Said the farmer, "Say no more,
But rest thee here at my cottage porch,
    For thy feet are weary and sore."

"I was with Grant"—the stranger said;
    Said the farmer, "Nay, no more,—
I prithee sit at my frugal board,
    And eat of my humble store.

"How fares my boy,—my soldier boy,
    Of the old Ninth Army Corps?
I warrant he bore him gallantly
    In the smoke and the battle's roar!"

"I know him not," said the aged man,
    "And, as I remarked before,
I was with Grant"—"Nay, nay, I know,"
    Said the farmer, "say no more:

"He fell in battle,—I see, alas!
    Thou'dst smooth these tidings o'er,—
Nay: speak the truth, whatever it be,
    Though it rend my bosom's core.

"How fell he,—with his face to the foe,
    Upholding the flag he bore?
Oh say not that my boy disgraced
    The uniform that he wore!"

"I cannot tell," said the aged man,
    "And should have remarked, before,
That I was with Grant, In Illinois,—
    Some three years before the war."

Then the farmer spake him never a word,
But beat with his fist full sore
That aged man, who had worked for Grant
Some three years before the war.

31.   *Plain Language from Truthful
James*

TABLE MOUNTAIN, 1870

WHICH I wish to remark,
    And my language is plain,
That for ways that are dark
    And for tricks that are vain,
The heathen Chinee is peculiar:
    Which the same I would rise to explain.

Ah Sin was his name;
    And I shall not deny,
In regard to the same,
    What that name might imply;
But his smile it was pensive and childlike.
    As I frequent remarked to Bill Nye.

It was August the third,
    And quite soft was the skies;
Which it might be inferred
    That Ah Sin was likewise;
Yet he played it that day upon William
    And me in a way I despise.

Which we had a small game,
    And Ah Sin took a hand:
It was Euchre. The same
    He did not understand;
But he smiled, as he sat by the table,
    With the smile that was childlike and bland.

60

FRANCIS BRET HARTE

Yet the cards they were stocked
  In a way that I grieve,
And my feelings were shocked
  At the state of Nye's sleeve,
Which was stuffed full of aces and bowers,
  And the same with intent to deceive.

But the hands that were played
  By that heathen Chinee,
And the points that he made,
  Were quite frightful to see,—
Till at last he put down a right bower,
  Which the same Nye had dealt unto me.

Then I looked up at Nye,
  And he gazed upon me;
And he rose with a sigh,
  And said, "Can this be?
We are ruined by Chinese cheap labor,"—
  And he went for that heathen Chinee.

In the scene that ensued
  I did not take a hand,
But the floor it was strewed,
  Like the leaves on the strand,
With the cards that Ah Sin had been hiding,
  In the game "he did not understand."

In his sleeves, which were long,
  He had twenty-four packs,—
Which was coming it strong,
  Yet I state but the facts;
And we found on his nails, which were taper,
  What is frequent in tapers,—that's wax.

Which is why I remark,
   And my language is plain,
That for ways that are dark,
   And for tricks that are vain,
The heathen Chinee is peculiar,—
   Which the same I am free to maintain.

32.   *From "John Burns of Gettysburg"*

JUST where the tide of battle turns,
   Erect and lonely, stood old John Burns.

In the antique vestments and long white hair,
The Past of the Nation in battle there;
And some of the soldiers since declare
That the gleam of his old white hat afar,
Like the crested plume of the brave Navarre,
That day was their oriflamme of war.

So raged the battle. You know the rest:
How the rebels, beaten and backward pressed,
Broke at the final charge and ran.
At which John Burns—a practical man—
Shouldered his rifle, unbent his brows,
And then went back to his bees and cows.

That is the story of old John Burns;
This is the moral the reader learns:
In fighting the battle, the question's whether
You'll show a hat that's white, or a feather!

EDWARD ROWLAND SILL

The Fool's Prayer

(1841–1887)

THE royal feast was done; the King
    Sought some new sport to banish care,
And to his jester cried: "Sir Fool,
    Kneel now, and make for us a prayer!"

The jester doffed his cap and bells,
    And stood the mocking court before;
They could not see the bitter smile
    Behind the painted grin he wore.

He bowed his head, and bent his knee
    Upon the monarch's silken stool;
His pleading voice arose: "O Lord,
    Be merciful to me, a fool!

"No pity, Lord, could change the heart
    From red with wrong to white as wool;
The rod must heal the sin: but Lord,
    Be merciful to me, a fool!

"'Tis not by guilt the onward sweep
    Of truth and right, O Lord, we stay;
'Tis by our follies that so long
    We hold the earth from heaven away.

"These clumsy feet, still in the mire,
    Go crushing blossoms without end;
These hard, well-meaning hands we thrust
    Among the heart-strings of a friend.

"The ill-timed truth we might have kept—
    Who knows how sharp it pierced and stung?
The word we had not sense to say—
    Who knows how grandly it had rung!

63

EDWARD ROWLAND SILL

"Our faults no tenderness should ask,
    The chastening stripes must cleanse them all;
But for our blunders—oh, in shame
    Before the eyes of heaven we fall.

"Earth bears no balsam for mistakes;
    Men crown the knave, and scourge the tool
That did his will; but Thou, O Lord,
    Be merciful to me, a fool!"

The room was hushed; in silence rose
    The King, and sought his gardens cool,
And walked apart, and murmured low,
    "Be merciful to me, a fool!"

CHARLES EDWARD CARRYL

34.   *Robinson Crusoe*

(1841–1920)

THE night was thick and hazy,
    When the Piccadilly Daisy
Carried down the crew and captain in the sea;
    And I think the water drowned 'em,
    For they never, never found 'em,
And I know they didn't come ashore with me.

Oh! 'twas very sad and lonely
    When I found myself the only
Population on this cultivated shore;
    But I've made a little tavern
    In a rocky little cavern,
And I sit and watch for people at the door.

I spent no time in looking
    For a girl to do my cooking,
As I'm quite a clever hand at making stews;
    But I had that fellow Friday

64

CHARLES EDWARD CARRYL

Just to keep the tavern tidy,
And to put a Sunday polish on my shoes.

I have a little garden
That I'm cultivating lard in,
As the things I eat are rather tough and dry;
For I live on toasted lizards,
Prickly pears, and parrot gizzards,
And I'm really very fond of beetle-pie.

The clothes I had were furry,
And it made me fret and worry
When I found the moths were eating off the hair;
And I had to scrape and sand 'em,
And I boiled 'em and I tanned 'em,
Till I got the fine morocco suit I wear.

I sometimes seek diversion
In a family excursion
With the few domestic animals you see;
And we take along a carrot
As refreshments for the parrot,
And a little can of jungleberry tea.

Then we gather as we travel
Bits of moss and dirty gravel,
And we chip off little specimens of stone;
And we carry home as prizes
Funny bugs of handy sizes,
Just to give the day a scientific tone.

If the roads are wet and muddy,
We remain at home and study,—
For the Goat is very clever at a sum,—
And the Dog, instead of fighting,
Studies ornamental writing,
While the Cat is taking lessons on the drum.

CHARLES EDWARD CARRYL

We retire at eleven,
And we rise again at seven;
And I wish to call attention, as I close,
To the fact that all the scholars
Are correct about their collars,
And particular in turning out their toes.

AMBROSE BIERCE

35.　　　　　*The Bride*

(1842-1914)

"YOU know, my friends, with what a brave
　　　carouse
I made a second marriage in my house,—
　　Divorced old barren Reason from my bed
And took the Daughter of the Vine to spouse."

So sang the Lord of Poets.　In a gleam
Of light that made her like an angel seem,
　　The Daughter of the Vine said: "I myself
Am Reason, and the Other was a Dream."

36.　　　　　*Another Way*

I LAY in silence, dead.　A woman came
　　And laid a rose upon my breast, and said,
"May God be merciful."　She spoke my name,
　　And added, "It is strange to think him dead.

"He loved me well enough, but 't was his way
　　To speak it lightly."　Then, beneath her breath:
"Besides"—I knew what further she would say,
　　But then a footfall broke my dream of death.

66

11140

AMBROSE BIERCE

To-day the words are mine. I lay the rose
  Upon her breast, and speak her name, and deem
It strange indeed that she is dead. God knows
  I had more pleasure in the other dream.

37.   *Creation*

GOD dreamed—the suns sprang flaming into place,
  And sailing worlds with many a venturous race.
He woke—His smile alone illumined space.

RICHARD WATSON GILDER

38.   *A Midsummer Song*
                                    (1844-1909)

O, FATHER'S gone to market-town, he was up
        before the day,
And Jamie's after robins, and the man is making hay,
And whistling down the hollow goes the boy that minds
    the mill,
While mother from the kitchen-door is calling with a
    will:
        "Polly!—Polly!—The cows are in the corn!
        O, where's Polly?"

From all the misty morning air there comes a summer
    sound—
A murmur as of waters from skies and trees and ground.
The birds they sing upon the wing, the pigeons bill and
    coo,
And over hill and hollow rings again the loud halloo:
        "Polly!—Polly!—The cows are in the corn!
        O, where's Polly!"

67

RICHARD WATSON GILDER

Above the trees the honey-bees swarm by with buzz
    and boom,
And in the field and garden a thousand blossoms bloom.
Within the farmer's meadow a brown-eyed daisy blows,
And down at the edge of the hollow a red and thorny
    rose.
      But Polly!—Polly!—The cows are in the corn!
      O, where's Polly?

How strange at such a time of day the mill should stop
    its clatter!
The farmer's wife is listening now and wonders what's
    the matter.
O, wild the birds are singing in the wood and on the hill,
While whistling up the hollow goes the boy that minds
    the mill.
      But Polly!—Polly!—The cows are in the corn!
      O, where's Polly?

JOHN BOYLE O'REILLY

39.   *In Bohemia*

(1844-1890)

I'D rather live in Bohemia than in any other land;
    For only there are the values true,
And the laurels gathered in all men's view,
The prizes of traffic and state are won
By shrewdness or force or by deeds undone;
But fame is sweeter without the feud,
And the wise of Bohemia are never shrewd.
Here, pilgrims stream with a faith sublime
From every class and clime and time,
Aspiring only to be enrolled
With the names that are writ in the book of gold;

68

JOHN BOYLE O'REILLY

And each one bears in mind or hand
A palm of the dear Bohemian land.
The scholar first, with his book—a youth
Aflame with the glory of harvested truth;
A girl with a picture, a man with a play,
A boy with a wolf he has modeled in clay;
A smith with a marvelous hilt and sword,
A player, a king, a plowman, a lord—
And the player is king when the door is past,
The plowman is crowned, and the lord is last!

I'd rather fail in Bohemia than win in another land;
There are no titles inherited there,
No hoard or hope for the brainless heir;
No gilded dullard native born
To stare at his fellow with leaden scorn:
Bohemia has none but adopted sons;
Its limits, where Fancy's bright stream runs;
Its honors, not garnered for thrift or trade,
But for beauty and truth men's souls have made.
To the empty heart in a jeweled breast
There is value, maybe, in a purchased crest;
But the thirsty of soul soon learn to know
The moistureless froth of the social show;
The vulgar sham of the pompous feast
Where the heaviest purse is the highest priest;
The organized charity, scrimped and iced,
In the name of a cautious, statistical Christ;
The smile restrained, the respectable cant,
When a friend in need is a friend in want;
Where the only aim is to keep afloat,
And a brother may drown with a cry in his throat.
Oh, I long for the glow of a kindly heart and the grasp
      of a friendly hand,
And I'd rather live in Bohemia than in any other land.

GEORGE THOMAS LANIGAN

40.   *A Threnody*
(1845-1886)

THE AHKOOND OF SWAT IS DEAD—*London Papers*

WHAT, what, what,
  What's the news from Swat?
 Sad news,
 Bad news,
Comes by the cable led
Through the Indian Ocean's bed,
Through the Persian Gulf, the Red
Sea and the Med-
Iterranean—he's dead;
The Ahkoond is dead!

For the Ahkoond I mourn,
  Who wouldn't?
He strove to disregard the message stern,
  But he Ahkoodn't.
Dead, dead, dead;
  (Sorrow, Swats!)
Swats wha hae wi' Ahkoond bled,
Swats whom he hath often led
Onward to a gory bed,
  Or to victory,
   As the case might be,
    Sorrow, Swats!
Tears shed,
  Shed tears like water.
Your great Ahkoond is dead!
  That Swats the matter!

Mourn, city of Swat!
Your great Ahkoond is not,
But lain 'mid worms to rot.
His mortal part alone, his soul **was caught**

70

GEORGE THOMAS LANIGAN

(Because he was a good Ahkoond)
Up to the bosom of Mahound.
Though earthy walls his frame surround
(Forever hallowed be the ground!)
And sceptics mock the lowly mound
And say "He's now of no Ahkoond!"
His soul is in the skies,—
The azure skies that bend above his loved
    Metropolis of Swat.
He sees with larger, other eyes,
Athwart all earthly mysteries—
He knows what's Swat.

Let Swat bury the great Ahkoond
  With a noise of mourning and of lamentation!
Let Swat bury the great Ahkoond
  With the noise of the mourning
    Of the Swattish nation!
    Fallen is at length
    Its tower of strength,
  Its sun is dimmed ere it had nooned;
  Dead lies the great Ahkoond,
    The great Ahkoond of Swat
    Is not!

JOSEPH I. C. CLARKE

41.   *The Fighting Race*

(1846–1925)

"READ out the names!" and Burke sat back,
  And Kelly drooped his head,
While Shea—they call him Scholar Jack—
  Went down the list of the dead.

JOSEPH I. C. CLARKE

Officers, seamen, gunners, marines,
　　The crews of the gig and yawl,
The bearded man and the lad in his teens,
　　Carpenters, coal-passers—all.
Then, knocking the ashes from out his pipe,
　　Said Burke in an offhand way:
"We're all in that dead man's list, by Cripe!
　　Kelly and Burke and Shea."
"Well, here's to the Maine, and I'm sorry for Spain,"
　　Said Kelly and Burke and Shea.

"Wherever there's Kellys there's trouble," said Burke.
　　"Wherever fighting's the game,
Or a spice of danger in grown man's work,"
　　Said Kelly, "you'll find my name."
"And do we fall short," said Burke, getting mad,
　　"When it's touch-and-go for life?"
Said Shea, "It's thirty-odd years, bedad,
　　Since I charged to drum and fife
Up Marye's Heights, and my old canteen
　　Stopped a rebel ball on its way;
There were blossoms of blood on our sprigs of green—
　　Kelly and Burke and Shea—
And the dead didn't brag." "Well, here's to the flag!"
　　Said Kelly and Burke and Shea.

"I wish 'twas in Ireland, for there's the place,"
　　Said Burke, "that we'd die by right,
In the cradle of our soldier race,
　　After one good stand-up fight.
My grandfather fell on Vinegar Hill,
　　And fighting was not his trade;
But his rusty pike's in the cabin still,
　　With Hessian blood on the blade."

JOSEPH I. C. CLARKE

"Aye, aye," said Kelly, "the pikes were great
   When the word was 'clear the way!'—
We were thick on the roll in ninety-eight—
   Kelly and Burke and Shea."
"Well, here's to the pike and the sword and the like!"
   Said Kelly and Burke and Shea.

And Shea, the scholar, with rising joy,
   Said, "We were at Ramillies;
We left our bones at Fontenoy
   And up in the Pyrenees;
Before Dunkirk, on Landen's plain,
   Cremona, Lille, and Ghent;
We're all over Austria, France, and Spain,
   Wherever they pitched a tent.
We've died for England from Waterloo
   To Egypt and Dargai;
And still there's enough for a corps or crew,
   Kelly and Burke and Shea."
"Well, here's to good honest fighting-blood!"
   Said Kelly and Burke and Shea.

"Oh, the fighting races don't die out,
   If they seldom die in bed,
For love is first in their hearts, no doubt,"
   Said Burke; then Kelly said:
"When Michael, the Irish Archangel, stands,
   The Angel with the sword,
And the battle-dead from a hundred lands
   Are ranged in one big horde,
Our line, that for Gabriel's trumpet waits,
   Will stretch three deep that day,
From Jehoshaphat to the Golden Gates—
   Kelly and Burke and Shea."
"Well, here's thank God for the race and the sod!"
   Said Kelly and Burke and Shea.

JAMES JEFFREY ROCHE

42.   *The V-a-s-e*

(1847-1908)

FROM the madding crowd they stand apart,
    The maidens four and the Work of Art;

And none might tell from sight alone
In which had Culture ripest grown,—

The Gotham Million fair to see,
The Philadelphia Pedigree,

The Boston Mind of azure hue,
Or the soulful Soul from Kalamazoo,—

For all loved Art in a seemly way,
With an earnest soul and a capital A.

.   .   .   .   .

Long they worshipped; but no one broke
The sacred stillness, until up spoke

The Western one from the nameless place,
Who blushing said: "What a lovely vace!"

Over three faces a sad smile flew,
And they edged away from Kalamazoo.

But Gotham's haughty soul was stirred
To crush the stranger with one small word.

Deftly hiding reproof in praise,
She cries: "'Tis, indeed, a lovely vaze!"

But brief her unworthy triumph when
The lofty one from the home of Penn,

With the consciousness of two grandpapas,
Exclaims: "It is quite a lovely vahs!"

And glances round with an anxious thrill,
Awaiting the word of Beacon Hill.

74

JAMES JEFFREY ROCHE

But the Boston maid smiles courteouslee,
And gently murmurs: "Oh pardon me!

"I did not catch your remark, because
I was so entranced with that charming vaws!"

> *Dies erit praegelida*
> *Sinistra quum Bostonia.*

JOEL CHANDLER HARRIS

43.   *The Plough-Hands' Song*

NIGGER mighty happy w'en he layin' by co'n—
    Dat sun 's a-slantin';
Nigger mighty happy w'en he year de dinner ho'n—
    Dat sun 's a-slantin';
En he mo' happy still w'en de night draws on—
    Dat sun's a-slantin';
Dat sun 's a-slantin' des ez sho's you bo'n!
En it's rise up, Primus! fetch anudder yell:
Dat ole dun cow des a-shakin' up 'er bell,
En de frogs chunin' up 'fo de jew done fell:
Good-night, Mr. Killdee! I wish you mighty well!—
    Mr. Kildee! I wish you mighty well!—
                  I wish you mighty well!

De c'on 'll be ready 'g'inst dumplin' day,
    Dat sun 's a-slantin';
But nigger gotter watch, en stick, en stay,
    Dat sun 's a-slantin';
Same ez de bee-martin watchin' un de jay,
    Dat sun 's a-slantin';
Dat sun 's a-slantin' en a-slippin' away!
Den it's rise up, Primus! en gin it t' um strong:

JOEL CHANDLER HARRIS

De cow's gwine home wid der ding-dang-dong;
Sling in anudder tech er de ole time song:
Good-night, Mr. Whipperwill! *don't stay long!—*
  Mr. Whipperwill! don't stay long!—
                                        Don't stay long!

De shadders, dey er creepin' todes de top er de hill,
  Dat sun 's a-slantin';
But night don't 'stroy w'at de day done buil',
  Dat sun 's a-slantin';
'Less de noddin' er de nigger give de ash-cake a chill—
  Dat sun 's a-slantin';
Dat sun's a-slantin' en slippin' down still!
Den sing it out, Primus! des holler en bawl,
En w'ilst we er strippin' deze mules fer de stall,
Let de gals ketch de soun' er de plantashun call:
Oh, it's good-night, ladies! my love unter you all!—
  Ladies! my love unter you all!—
                                        My love unter you all!

EUGENE FIELD

44. *The Truth About Horace*

(1850–1895)

IT is very aggravating
  To hear the solemn prating
Of the fossils who are stating
  That old Horace was a prude;
When we know that with the ladies
He was always raising Hades,
And with many an escapade his
  Best productions are imbued.

EUGENE FIELD

There's really not much harm in a
Large number of his carmina,
But these people find alarm in a
    Few records of his acts;
So they'd squelch the muse caloric,
And to students sophomoric
They'd present as metaphoric
    What old Horace meant for facts.

We have always thought 'em lazy;
Now we adjudge 'em crazy!
Why, Horace was a daisy
    That was very much alive!
And the wisest of us know him
As his Lydia verses show him,—
Go, read that virile poem,—
    It is No. 25.

He was a very owl, sir,
And starting out to prowl, sir,
You bet he made Rome howl, sir,
    Until he filled his date;
With a massic-laden ditty
And a classic maiden pretty
He painted up the city,
    And Mæcenas paid the freight!

45.   *Apple-Pie and Cheese*

FULL many a sinful notion
        Conceived of foreign powers
Has come across the ocean
    To harm this land of ours;

EUGENE FIELD

And heresies called fashions
   Have modesty effaced,
And baleful, morbid passions
   Corrupt our native taste.
O tempora! O mores!
   What profanations these
That seek to dim the glories
   Of apple-pie and cheese!

I'm glad my education
   Enables me to stand
Against the vile temptation
   Held out on every hand;
Eschewing all the tittles
   With vanity replete,
I'm loyal to the victuals
   Our grandsires used to eat!
I'm glad I've got three willing boys
   To hang around and tease
Their mother for the filling joys
   Of apple-pie and cheese!

Your flavored creams and ices
   And your dainty angel-food
Are mighty fine devices
   To regale the dainty dude;
Your terrapin and oysters,
   With wine to wash 'em down,
Are just the thing for roisters
   When painting of the town;
No flippant, sugared notion
   Shall *my* appetite appease,
Or bate my soul's devotion
   To apple-pie and cheese!

EUGENE FIELD

The pie my Julia makes me
  (God bless her Yankee ways!)
On memory's pinions takes me
  To dear Green Mountain days;
And seems like I saw Mother
  Lean on the window-sill,
A-handin' me and brother
  What she knows 'll keep us still;
And these feelings are so grateful,
  Says I, "Julia, if you please,
I'll take another plateful
  Of that apple-pie and cheese!"

And cheese! No alien it, sir,
  That's brought across the sea,—
No Dutch antique, nor Switzer,
  Nor glutinous de Brie;
There's nothing I abhor so
  As mawmets of this ilk—
Give *me* the harmless morceau
  That's made of true-blue milk!
No matter what conditions
  Dyspeptic come to feaze,
The best of all physicians
  Is apple-pie and cheese!

Though ribalds may decry 'em,
  For these twin boons we stand,
Partaking thrice per diem
  Of their fulness out of hand;
No enervating fashion
  Shall cheat us of our right
To gratify our passion
  With a mouthful at a bite!

We'll cut it square or bias,
  Or any way we please,

EUGENE FIELD

And faith shall justify us
　When we carve our pie and cheese!

De gustibus, 't is stated,
　Non disputandum est.
Which meaneth, when translated,
　That all is for the best.
So let the foolish choose 'em
　The vapid sweets of sin,
I will not disabuse 'em
　Of the heresy they're in;
But I, when I undress me
　Each night, upon my knees
Will ask the Lord to bless me
　With apple-pie and cheese!

46.　　　　　　*Horace to Pyrrha*

WHAT perfumed, posie-dizened sirrah,
　　With smiles for diet,
Clasps you, O fair but faithless Pyrrha,
　On the quiet?
For whom do you bind up your tresses,
　As spun-gold yellow,—
Meshes that go, with your caresses,
　To snare a fellow?

How will he rail at fate capricious,
　And curse you duly!
Yet now he deems your wiles delicious,
　You perfect, truly!
Pyrrha, your love's a treacherous ocean;
　He'll soon fall in there!
Then shall I gloat on his commotion,
　For *I* have been there!

47.   *The Old Man and Jim*

(1853–1916)

OLD man never had much to say—
    'Ceptin' to Jim,—
And Jim was the wildest boy he had—
    And the Old man jes' wrapped up in him!
Never heerd him speak but once
Er twice in my life,—and first time was
When the army broke out, and Jim he went,
The Old man backin' him, fer three months.—
And all 'at I heerd the Old man say
Was, jes' as we turned to start away,—
    "Well; good-bye, Jim:
        Take keer of yourse'f!"

'Peard-like, he was more satisfied
    Jes' *lookin'* at Jim,
And likin' him all to hisse'f-like, see?—
    'Cause he was jes' wrapped up in him!
And over and over I mind the day
The Old man come and stood round in the way
While we was drillin', a-watchin' Jim—
And down at the deepot a-heerin' him say,—
    "Well; good-bye, Jim:
        Take keer of yourse'f!"

Never was nothin' about the farm
    Disting'ished Jim;—
Neighbours all ust to wonder why
    The Old man 'peared wrapped up in him:
But when Cap. Biggler, he writ back,
'At Jim was the bravest boy we had
In the whole dern rigiment, white er black,
And his fightin' good as his farmin' bad—
'At he had led, with a bullet clean
Bored through his thigh, and carried the flag

Through the bloodiest battle you ever seen,—
The Old man wound up a letter to him
'At Cap. read to us, 'at said,—"Tell Jim
  Good-bye;
    And take keer of hisse'f."

Jim come back jes' long enough
  To take the whim
'At he'd like to go back in the cavelry—
  And the Old man jes' wrapped up in him!—
Jim 'lowed 'at he'd had sich luck afore,
Guessed he'd tackle her three years more.
And the Old man give him a colt he'd raised
And follered him over to Camp Ben Wade,
And laid around fer a week er so,
Watchin' Jim on dress-parade—
Tel finally he rid away,
And last he heerd was the Old man say,—
    "Well; good-bye, Jim:
      Take keer of yourse'f!"

Tuk the papers, the Old man did,
  A-watchin' fer Jim—
Fully believin' he'd make his mark
  Some way—jes' wrapped up in him!—
And many a time the word 'u'd come
'At stirred him up like the tap of a drum—
At Petersburg, fer instance, where
Jim rid right into their cannons there,
And tuk 'em, and p'inted 'em t'other way,
And socked it home to the boys in grey,
As they skooted fer timber, and on and on—
Jim a lieutenant and one arm gone,
And the Old man's words in his mind all day,—
    "Well; good-bye, Jim:
      Take keer of yourse'f!"

JAMES WHITCOMB RILEY

Think of a private, now, perhaps,
   We'll say like Jim,
'At's clumb clean up to the shoulder-straps—
   And the Old man jes' wrapped up in him!
Think of him—with the war plum' through,
And the glorious old Red-White-and-Blue
A-laughin' the news down over Jim,
And the Old man, bendin' over him—
The surgeon turnin' away with tears
'At hadn't leaked fer years and years—
As the hand of the dyin' boy clung to
His father's, the old voice in his ears,—
   "Well; good-bye, Jim:
      Take keer of yourse'f!"

IRWIN RUSSELL

48.   *The First Banjo*

(1853-1879)

G O 'way, fiddle; folks is tired o' hearin' you a-
   squawkin'—
Keep silence fur yo' betters!—don't you heah de banjo
   talkin'?
About de 'possum's tail she's gwine to lecter—ladies,
   listen!—
About de ha'r whut isn't dar, an' why de ha'r is missin':

"Dar's gwine to be a' oberflow," said Noah, lookin'
   solemn—
Fur Noah tuk the "*Herald*," an' he read de ribber
   column—
An' so he sot his hands to wuk a-cl'arin' timber-
   patches,
An' 'lowed he's gwine to build a boat to beat de steamah
   Natchez.

Ol' Noah kep' a-nailin' an' a-chippin' an' a-sawin';
An' all de wicked neighbours kep' a-laughin' an' a-
pshawin';
But Noah didn't min' 'em, knowin' whut wuz gwine to
happen:
An' forty days an' forty nights de rain it kep' a-drap-
pin'.

Now, Noah had done cotched a lot ob ebry sort o'
beas'es—
Ob all de shows a-trabbelin', it beat 'em all to pieces!
He had a Morgan colt an' sebral head o' Jarsey cattle—
An' druv 'em 'board de Ark as soon 's he heered de
thunder rattle.

Den sech anoder fall ob rain!—it come so awful hebby,
De ribber riz immejitly, an' busted troo de lebbee;
De people all wuz drownded out—'cep' Noah an' de
critters,
An' men he'd hired to work de boat—an' one to mix de
bitters.

De Ark she kep' a-sailin' an' a-sailin', *an'* a-sailin';
De lion got his dander up, an' like to bruk de palin';
De sarpints hissed; de painters yelled; tell, whut wid
all de fussin',
You c'u'dn't hardly heah de mate a-bossin' roun' an'
cussin'.

Now, Ham, de only nigger whut wuz runnin' on de
packet,
Got lonesome in de barber-shop, and c'u'dn't stan' de
racket;
84

An' so, fur to amuse he-se'f, he steamed some wood an'
bent it,
An' soon he had a banjo made—de fust dat wuz in-
vented.

He wet de ledder, stretched it on; made bridge an'
screws an' aprin;
An' fitted in a proper neck—'twas berry long and tap-
'rin';
He tuk some tin, an' twisted him a thimble fur to ring it;
An' den de mighty question riz: how wuz he gwine to
string it?

De 'possum had as fine a tail as dis dat I's a-singin';
De ha'r's so long an' thick an' strong,—des fit fur
banjo-stringin';
Dat nigger shaved 'em off as short as wash-day dinner
graces;
An' sorted ob 'em by de size, f'om little E's to basses.

He strung her, tuned her, struck a jig,—'twus "Nebber
min' de wedder,"—
She soun' like forty-lebben bands a-playin' all togedder;
Some went to pattin'; some to dancin': Noah called de
figgers;
An' Ham he sot an' knocked de tune, de happiest ob
niggers!

Now, sence dat time—it's mighty strange—dere's not
de slightes' showin'
Ob any ha'r at all upon de 'possum's tail a-growin';
An' curi's, too, dat nigger's ways: his people nebber
los' 'em—
Fur whar you finds de nigger—dar's de banjo an' de
'possum!

HENRY CUYLER BUNNER

49.   *Behold the Deeds!*

CHANT ROYAL

*Being the Plaint of Adolphe Culpepper Ferguson, Sales-
man of Fancy Notions, held in durance of his Landlady
for a failure to connect on Saturday night.*

I

I WOULD that all men my hard case might know;
   How grievously I suffer for no sin:
I, Adolphe Culpepper Ferguson, for lo!
   I, of my landlady am lockèd in.
For being short on this sad Saturday,
Nor having shekels of silver wherewith to pay,
She has turned and is departed with my key;
Wherefore, not even as other boarders free,
   I sing (as prisoners to their dungeon stones
When for ten days they expiate a spree):
   Behold the deeds that are done of Mrs. Jones!

II

One night and one day have I wept my woe;
   Nor wot I when the morrow doth begin,
If I shall have to write to Briggs & Co.,
   To pray them to advance the requisite tin
For ransom of their salesman, that he may
Go forth as other boarders go alway—
As those I hear now flocking from their tea,
Led by the daughter of my landlady
   Pianoward. This day for all my moans,
Dry bread and water have been servèd me.
   Behold the deeds that are done of Mrs. Jones!

III

Miss Amabel Jones is musical, and so
   The heart of the young he-boarder doth win,
86

HENRY CUYLER BUNNER

Playing "The Maiden's Prayer," adagio—
  That fetcheth him, as fetcheth the bunco skin
The innocent rustic. For my part, I pray:
That Badarjewska maid may wait for aye
Ere sits she with a lover, as did we
Once sit together, Amabel! Can it be
  That all of that arduous wooing not atones
For Saturday shortness of trade dollars three?
  Behold the deeds that are done of Mrs. Jones!

IV

Yea! she forgets the arm was wont to go
  Around her waist. She wears a buckle whose pin
Galleth the crook of the young man's elbow;
  I forget not, for I that youth have been.
Smith was aforetime the Lothario gay.
Yet once, I mind me, Smith was forced to stay
Close in his room. Not calm, as I, was he;
But his noise brought no pleasaunce, verily.
  Small ease he gat of playing on the bones,
Or hammering on his stove-pipe, that I see.
  Behold the deeds that are done of Mrs. Jones!

V

Thou, for whose fear the figurative crow
  I eat, accursed be thou and all thy kin!
Thee will I show up—yea, up will I show
  Thy too thick buckwheats, and they tea too thin.
Ay! here I dare thee, ready for the fray!
Thou dost not keep a first-class house, I say!
It does not with the advertisements agree.
Thou lodgest a Briton with a pugaree,
  And thou has harbored Jacobses and Cohns,
Also a Mulligan. Thus denounce I thee!
  Behold the deeds that are done of Mrs. Jones!

ENVOY

Boarders! the worst I have not told to ye:
She hath stole my trousers, that I may not flee
Privily by the window. Hence these groans,
There is no fleeing in a *robe de nuit*.
Behold the deeds that are done of Mrs. Jones!

TUDOR JENKS

50.   *An Old Bachelor*

(1857–1922)

'TWAS raw, and chill, and cold outside,
     With a boisterous wind untamed,
But I was sitting snug within,
     Where my good log-fire flamed.
         As my clock ticked,
         My cat purred,
         And my kettle sang.

I read me a tale of war and love,
     Brave knights and their ladies fair;
And I brewed a brew of stiff hot-scotch
     To drive away dull care.
         As my clock ticked,
         My cat purred,
         And my kettle sang.

At last the candles sputtered out,
     But the embers still were bright,
When I turned my tumbler upside down,
     An' bade m'self g' night!
         As th' ket'l t-hic-ked,
         The clock purred,
         And the cat (hic) sang!

FRANK LEBBY STANTON

51.   *A Plantation Ditty*

(1857–

DE gray owl sing fum de chimbly top:
    "Who—who—is—you-oo?"
En I say: "Good Lawd, hit's des po' me,
En I ain't quite ready fer de Jasper Sea;
I'm po' en sinful, en you 'lowed I'd be;
    Oh, wait, good Lawd, 'twell ter-morror!"

De gray owl sing fum de cypress tree:
    "Who—who—is—you-oo?"
En I say: "Good Lawd, ef you look you'll see
Hit ain't nobody but des po' me,
En I like ter stay 'twell my time is free;
    Oh, wait, good Lawd, 'twell ter-morror!"

52.   *The Graveyard Rabbit*

IN the white moonlight, where the willow waves,
    He halfway gallops among the graves—
A tiny ghost in the gloom and gleam,
Content to dwell where the dead men dream,

But wary still!
For they plot him ill;
For the graveyard rabbit hath a charm
(May God defend us!) to shield from harm.

Over the shimmering slabs he goes—
Every grave in the dark he knows;
But his nest is hidden from human eye
Where headstones broken on old graves lie.

Wary still!
For they plot him ill;
For the graveyard rabbit, though sceptics scoff,
Charmeth the witch and the wizard off!

FRANK LEBBY STANTON

The black man creeps, when the night is dim,
Fearful, still, on the track of him;
Or fleetly follows the way he runs,
For he heals the hurts of the conjured ones.

Wary still!
For they plot him ill;
The soul's bewitched that would find release,—
To the graveyard rabbit go for peace!

He holds their secret—he brings a boon
Where winds moan wild in the dark o' the moon;
And gold shall glitter and love smile sweet
To whoever shall sever his furry feet!

Wary still!
For they plot him ill;
For the graveyard rabbit hath a charm
(May God defend us!) to shield from harm.

SAM WALTER FOSS

53. *The Prayer of Cyrus Brown*

(1858–1911)

"THE proper way for a man to pray,"
  Said Deacon Lemuel Keyes,
"And the only proper attitude
  Is down upon his knees."

"No, I should say the way to pray,"
  Said Rev. Doctor Wise,
"Is standing straight with outstretched arms
  And rapt and upturned eyes."

SAM WALTER FOSS

"Oh, no; no, no," said Elder Slow,
  "Such posture is too proud:
A man should pray with eyes fast closed
  And head contritely bowed."

"It seems to me his hands should be
  Austerely clasped in front,
With both thumbs pointing toward the ground,"
  Said Rev. Doctor Blunt.

"Las' year I fell in Hodgkin's well
  Head first," said Cyrus Brown,
"With both my heels a-stickin' up,
  My head a-pinting down;

"An' I made a prayer right then an' there—
  Best prayer I ever said,
The prayingest prayer I ever prayed,
  A-standing on my head."

ERNEST LAWRENCE THAYER

54.   *Casey at the Bat*

(1863-   )

THE outlook wasn't brilliant for the Mudville nine
    that day;
The score stood four to two, with but one inning more to
    play;
And so, when Cooney died at first, and Burrows did the
    same,
A sickly silence fell upon the patrons of the game.

A straggling few got up to go in deep despair. The rest
Clung to the hope which springs eternal in the human
     breast;
They thought, if only Casey could but get a whack, at
     that,
They'd put up even money now, with Casey at the bat.

But Flynn preceded Casey, as did also Jimmy Blake,
And the former was a pudding and the latter was a fake;
So upon that stricken multitude grim melancholy sat,
For there seemed but little chance of Casey's getting
     to the bat.

But Flynn let drive a single, to the wonderment of all,
And Blake, the much despisèd, tore the cover off the
     ball;
And when the dust had lifted, and they saw what had
     occurred,
There was Jimmy safe on second, and Flynn a-hugging
     third.

Then from the gladdened multitude went up a joyous
     yell,
It bounded from the mountain-top, and rattled in the
     dell;
It struck upon the hillside, and recoiled upon the flat;
For Casey, mighty Casey, was advancing to the bat.

There was ease in Casey's manner as he stepped into his
     place,
There was pride in Casey's bearing, and a smile on
     Casey's face;
And when, responding to the cheers, he lightly doffed
     his hat,
No stranger in the crowd could doubt 'twas Casey at
     the bat.

ERNEST LAWRENCE THAYER

Ten thousand eyes were on him as he rubbed his hands
    with dirt,
Five thousand tongues applauded when he wiped them
    on his shirt;
Then while the writhing pitcher ground the ball into
    his hip,
Defiance gleamed in Casey's eye, a sneer curled Casey's
    lip.

And now the leather-covered. sphere came hurtling
    through the air,
And Casey stood a-watching it in haughty grandeur
    there;
Close by the sturdy batsman the ball unheeded sped.
"That ain't my style," said Casey. "Strike one," the
    umpire said.

From the benches, black with people, there went up a
    muffled roar,
Like the beating of the storm-waves on a stern and
    distant shore;
"Kill him! kill the umpire!" shouted some one on the
    stand.
And it's likely they'd have killed him had not Casey
    raised his hand.

With a smile of Christian charity great Casey's visage
    shone;
He stilled the rising tumult; he bade the game go on;
He signalled to the pitcher, and once more the spheroid
    flew,
But Casey still ignored it, and the umpire said, "Strike
    two."

ERNEST LAWRENCE THAYER

"Fraud!" cried the maddened thousands, and the echo
  answered, "Fraud!"
But a scornful look from Casey, and the audience was
  awed;
They saw his face grow stern and cold, they saw his
  muscles strain,
And they knew that Casey would'nt let that ball go
  by again.

The sneer is gone from Casey's lips, his teeth are
  clenched in hate,
He pounds with cruel violence his bat upon the plate;
And now the pitcher holds the ball, and now he lets it go,
And now the air is shattered by the force of Casey's
  blow.

Oh! somewhere in this favored land the sun is shining
  bright,
The band is playing somewhere, and somewhere hearts
  are light;
And somewhere men are laughing, and somewhere
  children shout,
But there is no joy in Mudville—mighty Casey has
  struck out.

RICHARD HOVEY

55.   *The Kavanagh*
                                              (1864-1900)

A STONE jug and a pewter mug,
      And a table set for three!
A jug and a mug at every place,
And a biscuit or two with Brie!

RICHARD HOVEY

Three stone jugs of Cruiskeen Lawn,
And a cheese like crusted foam!
The Kavanagh receives to-night!
McMurrough is at home!

We three and the barley-bree!
And a health to the one away,
Who drifts down careless Italy,
God's wanderer and estray!
For friends are more than Arno's store
Of garnered charm, and he
Were blither with us here the night
Than Titian bids him be.

Throw ope the window to the stars,
And let the warm night in!
Who knows what revelry in Mars
May rhyme with rouse akin?
Fill up and drain the loving cup
And leave no drop to waste!
The moon looks in to see what's up—
Begad, she'd like a taste!

What odds if Leinster's kingly roll
Be now an idle thing?
The world is his who takes his toll,
A vagrant or a king.
What though the crown be melted down,
And the heir a gypsy roam?
The Kavanagh receives to-night!
McMurrough is at home!

We three and the barley-bree!
And the moonlight on the floor!
Who were a man to do with less?
What emperor has more?

RICHARD HOVEY

Three stone jugs of Cruiskeen Lawn,
And three stout hearts to drain
A slanter to the truth in the heart of youth
And the joy of the love of men.

BERT LESTON TAYLOR

56.* *The Dinosaur*

(1866–1921)

BEHOLD the mighty Dinosaur,
   Famous in prehistoric lore,
Not only for his weight and strength
But for his intellectual length.
You will observe by these remains
The creature had two sets of brains—
One in his head (the usual place),
The other at his spinal base.
Thus he could reason *a priori*
As well as *a posteriori*.
No problem bothered him a bit:
He made both head and tail of it.
So wise he was, so wise and solemn,
Each thought filled just a spinal column.
If one brain found the pressure strong
It passed a few ideas along;
If something slipped his forward mind
'Twas rescued by the one behind;
And if in error he was caught
He had a saving afterthought.
As he thought twice before he spoke
He had no judgments to revoke;
For he could think, without congestion,
Upon both sides of every question.

Oh, gaze upon this model beast,
Defunct ten million years at least.

BERT LESTON TAYLOR

Old Stuff

IF I go to see the play,
    Of the story I am certain;
Promptly it gets under way
    With the lifting of the curtain.
Builded all that's said and done
    On the ancient recipe—
'Tis the same old Two and One:
    A and B in love with C.

If I read the latest book,
    There's the mossy situation;
One may confidently look
    For the trite triangulation.
Old as time, but ever new,
    Seemingly, this tale of Three—
Same old yarn of One and Two:
    A and C in love with B.

If I cast my eyes around,
    Far and near and middle distance,
Still the formula is found
    In our everyday existence.
Everywhere I look I see—
    Fact or fiction, life or play—
Still the little game of Three:
    B and C in love with A.

While the ancient law fulfills,
    Myriad moons shall wane and wax.
Jack must have his pair of Jills,
    Jill must have her pair of Jacks.

58.   *Behind the Door*

HITHER, thither, little feet
    Patter on the floor;
Still am I in my retreat,
    Hid behind the door.

If my hiding-place is guessed,
    Comes a gleeful cry;
But if vain should be the quest,
    There are tears to dry.

      .   .   .   .

In the House of Life, my dear,
    All is not so fair;
Happiness is hiding here,
    Sorrow hiding there.

May the gods your life endow
    From their boundless store!
May you always find, as now,
    Love behind the door.

KATHARINE LEE BATES

59.   *Splendid Isolation*

A MORAL FROM LEXINGTON, 1775

OH, but my husband, Matthew,
    Was a slip from a crab apple tree!
Laughed when we women would punish
    King George by giving up tea!
    (How I missed my cup of Bohea!)

KATHARINE LEE BATES

"So I have my sling in the morning,
  My blackstrap at noon," said he,
"And my toddy at night, you'll not see me fight
  For the sake of a swallow of tea.
  What does it matter to me?"

The neighbors pointed the finger,
  But he only chuckled to see.
Not even with Parson Jonas Clarke
  Would my contrary man agree.
When Parson thundered against the Five
  Intolerable Acts
Till the meeting-house hummed like an angry hive,
Matthew would mutter: "I'm still alive,
  And my arms and legs are free.
  What does it matter to me?"

That Tuesday I had been brewing
  A fresh lot of beer for the flip
That Matthew will gulp by the mugful,
  While of tea I have never a sip.
  (But we've got King George on the hip!)
I'd been baking and sanding and scouring,
  So I lighted a tallow dip
Tired bones to balm with a blessed psalm,
  When a knock sent Rhoda, our slip
  Of a lass, to the door with a skip.

But her face that had been so rosy
  —And all for a lad in his teens—
Went white as she saw three strangers stand,
  Their cloaks drawn close for screens.
A whisk of wind, and the moonlight showed
  Flecks of the hated red.

KATHARINE LEE BATES

Without a word those tall shapes strode
To our great brick oven; they stole its load
  And back into darkness fled
  With our supper of beans and brown bread.

The lobsters! I hope their noses
  Were burned on the beanpot rim.
Home came my hungry Matthew,
  His mouth uncommonly grim
  As I told my tale with a vim.
He stooped with the flickering candle
  To that oven empty and dim,
Then rose and sprung where his flintlock hung,
  A patriot up to the brim!
  At last it mattered to him.

SAM S. STINSON

60.   *Nothin' Done*

                                   (1868–   )

WINTER is too cold fer work.
  Freezin' weather makes me shirk.

Spring comes on an' finds me wishin'
I could end my days a-fishin'.

Then in Summer, when it's hot,
I say work kin go to pot.

Autumn days, so calm an' hazy,
Kinda sorta make me lazy.

That's the way the seasons run.
Seems I can't git nothin' done.

EDWIN ARLINGTON ROBINSON

61.   *Miniver Cheevy*

(1869–   )

MINIVER CHEEVY, child of scorn,
   Grew lean while he assailed the seasons;
He wept that he was ever born,
   And he had reasons.

Miniver loved the days of old
   When swords were bright and steeds were prancing;
The vision of a warrior bold
   Would set him dancing.

Miniver sighed for what was not,
   And dreamed, and rested from his labors;
He dreamed of Thebes and Camelot,
   And Priam's neighbors.

Miniver mourned the ripe renown
   That made so many a name so fragrant;
He mourned Romance, now on the town,
   And Art, a vagrant.

Miniver loved the Medici,
   Albeit he had never seen one;
He would have sinned incessantly
   Could he have been one.

Miniver cursed the commonplace,
   And eyed a khaki suit with loathing;
He missed the medieval grace
   Of iron clothing.

Miniver scorned the gold he sought,
   But sore annoyed was he without it;
Miniver thought, and thought, and thought,
   And thought about it.

EDWIN ARLINGTON ROBINSON

Miniver Cheevy, born too late,
   Scratched his head and kept on thinking;
Miniver coughed, and called it fate,
   And kept on drinking.

STRICKLAND W. GILLILAN

62.   *A Dixie Lullaby*

(1869-)

LAUGHIN' wif yo' dinneh in de cohneh ob yo'
    mouf—
Sweetes' pickaninny in dis po'tion ob de Souf.
Lookin' at yo' mammy fum de tail-eend ob yo' eye—
Make has'e dar, brack baby, fo' yo' meal-time slippin'
    by.
Make dem sof' lips wiggle—yo's a triflin' li'l coon!
Mammy up en take yo' dinneh fum yo', putty soon!

Laughin' wif yo' dinneh in de cohneh ob yo' mouf—
Yo' ain't fear'd de crops will fail en ain't askeered o'
    drouf.
Rollin' roun' dem shiny eyes at mammy—li'l scamp!
Mammy she ain't lub yo' none—she fling yo' ter a
    tramp!
Huh-uh! Nee'n't pucker up yo' baby lips en cry!
Mammy gwine ter lub yo' twell de salty sea run dry.

Sleepin' wif his dinneh in de cohneh ob his mouf—
Wahm lips on de proudest mammy boozum in de Souf.
Belly full o' dinneh en his skeer all druv away—
Lawd! Huccome dey cain't stay small fohebeh en a
    day?
Bofe dem shiny windehs got dey shettahs farstened
    down—
Fix dat baid, Sis' Lindy, w'ile he slumbehin' so soun'!

102

ARTHUR GUITERMAN

63. *This is She*

(1871–   )

ON order that must be obeyed
   I sing of a dear little maid;
   A mirthfully serious,
   Sober, delirious,
   Gently imperious
      Maid.

And first we'll consider her eyes
(Alike as to color and size);
   Her winkable, blinkable,
   Merrily twinkable,
   Simply unthinkable
      Eyes.

Then, having a moment to spare,
We turn our attention to hair;
   Her tendrilly-curlative,
   Tumbly-and-whirlative,
   Super-superlative
      Hair.

Forbear to dismiss with a shrug
Her nose, undeniably pug;—
   Her strictly permissible,
   Turn-up-like-thisable,
   Urgently kissable
      Pug.

Now, moving a point to the south,
We come to an Actual Mouth;
   A coral, pearliferous,
   Argumentiferous,
   Mainly melliferous
      Mouth.

Observe, underneath it, a chin,
Connoting the dimple within;
  A steady, reliable,
  Hardly defiable,
  True, undeniable
    Chin.

By all that is fair! it appears
We'd almost forgotten her ears!
  Those never neglectable,
  Tinted, delectable,
  Highly respectable
    Ears!

And last let us speak of herself,
That blithe little gipsy and elf,
  Her quite unignorable,
  Absence-deplorable,
  Wholly adorable
    Self.

64.   *The Irreverent Brahmin*

A HINDU TRACT

A BRAHMIN, fat and debonair,
  Denied the Potency of Prayer!

"Absurd!" he scoffed, "to say that Gods
At ease on high would stoop to Clods

"And heed our million warring Prayers
To regulate our small Affairs!"

ARTHUR GUITERMAN

This Dogmatist of early days
Was lost within a jungle's maze,

Where, wildly ranging wide about
To find a pathway leading out,

Upon a Forest Godling's Shrine
He chanced, o'erhung with leaf and vine,

And—wonder! horror!—crouching there
A mighty Tiger, bowed in prayer!

(Tail curled, as may be well supposed,
Paws folded, eyes devoutly closed.)

"Strong God," he heard the Tiger say,
"I pray thee, send to me a Prey!"

The trustful Tiger closed his Prayer.—
Behold! a Brahmin trembling there!

The Brahmin never scoffed a whit.
The Prayer had Answer—*He* was *It*.

65.   *The Poem on Spring*

GREAT ALI, the Sultan, I've heard—
        (Please attend to my proem!),
Was shrewd as the serpent—aye, Solon to him was a
        dunce;
    Who else could repeat every word
        Of a sermon, a poem,
Or any old thing that was spoken before him but once?

ARTHUR GUITERMAN

While Eben al Hamid, his short
    Ethiopic attendant
And factum factotum, they say could repeat in a trice
    The plea of a lawyer in court
      For a guilty defendant,
Or President's Message (perhaps), if he heard it but
    twice.

Whenever a bard would intone
    An original sonnet
(For Sultans, you know, are the prey of the metrical
    bore),
    "That's ancient," the Ruler would groan,
      "As Mehitable's bonnet!
Now listen, and see for yourself that I've heard it
    before."

Whereat he would echo each phrase
    With precision emphatic;
And Eben, in turn, would repeat, never missing a
    rhyme;
    The poet would slink in a daze
      To his sorrowful attic,
While Eben and Ali would laugh for a week at a time.

Then Ali proclaimed in his pride:
    "For reward I will measure
The weight of that poem in gold which is proved to be
    new."
    And many a balladist tried
      For that fistful of treasure;
But penniless, puzzled, and shamed every singer with-
    drew.

ARTHUR GUITERMAN

At length came a minstrel of guile.
   (From the West, so I fear me);
He tinkled his merry guitar and addressed him to sing:
   "Your Highness," quoth he with a smile,
      "Will it please ye to hear me?
I've something that's Purely Unique—'tis a Poem on
      Spring.—

   "A Genuine Triumph of Mind
      That is urgently needed
By seventeen best magazines. Have I leave to begin?"
   "Proceed," sighed the Sultan, resigned;
      And the Minstrel proceeded
To startle the court with this Chant of Original Sin:

   "'Tis Spring on the lily-white leas
      Of the Forest of Arden!
'Tis Spring! and the blossoms appear and the leveret
      plays;
   The butterflies drift on the breeze
      To the elf-haunted garden;
The birdies of meadow and grove are rehearsing their
      lays.

   "'Bo-peep! Hullychee!' sings the Flick;
      'Korry-boo!' moans the Chitter;
'Quee-boggle-chee-pilli-moran!' sobs the Killikoloo.
   'Ping-pong! Watchi-toodle-kerwick!'
      All the Merimees twitter.
The Niblick avers, 'Kalli-bosh, taradiddle, koroo.'

   "'Go-dum, bally-hoosh!' is the note
      Of the Icthyosaurus,
'Notórum-dorando!' the blithe Hippocampus replies;

'Chim-chim-orizàba-pelote!'
    Rings the jubilant chorus
Of sweet Pterodactyls that wing the cerulean skies.

    "'The Kiddle observes to his mate,
    'Borum-àgo-majellum,
Elań, rododacktylos bree.' While the somnolent Bruff
    Ascends to the heavenly gate
    Chanting, 'Ho! Parabellum
Enteuthen—'" "Help! Stop! Oh, my head!" cried
    the Sultan; "Enough!

    "I've echoed queer words, I admit,
    All your brotherhood downing;
But who could repeat these uncivilized sounds you
    have made!
    Your poem should make quite a hit
    With the students of Browning—
So bring in your Manuscript, friend, and the gold shall
    be weighed."

    The Poet went forth, and returned
    With his holiday sash on,
Propelling a cart with a load of the heaviest brick
    On which he had graven and burned,
    Babylonian fashion,
The "words" of his poem!—a mean, reprehensible
    trick!

    The Sultan, demurring, 'tis true,
    Made an end by bestowing
The weight of that poem in gold,—a prodigious expense.
    And this have I sung unto you
    For the purpose of showing
*That even Spring Poets may manifest hard common
    sense!*
    108

T. A. DALY

66.   *The Blossomy Barrow*

ANTONIO SARTO ees buildin' a wall,
    But maybe he nevva gon' feenish at all.
  Eet sure won'ta be
  Teell flower an' tree
An' all kinda growin' theengs sleep een da Fall.

You see, deesa 'Tonio always ees want'
To leeve on a farm, so he buy wan las' mont'.
I s'posa som' day eet be verra nice place,
But shape dat he find eet een sure ees "deesgrace;"
Eet's busta so bad he must feexin' eet all,
An' firs' theeng he starta for build ees da wall.
Mysal' I go outa for see heem wan day,
An' dere I am catcha heem sweatin' away;
He's liftin' beeg stones from all parts of hees land
An' takin' dem up to da wall een hees hand!
I say to heem: "Tony, why don'ta you gat
Som' leetla wheel-barrow for halp you weeth dat?"

"O! com' an' I show you w'at's matter," he said,
An' so we go look at hees tools een da shed.
Dere's fina beeg wheel-barrow dere on da floor,
But w'at do you s'pose? From een under da door
Som' mornin'-glor' vines have creep eento da shed,
An' beautiful flower, all purpla an' red,
Smile out from da vina so pretty an' green
Dat tweest round da wheel an' da sides da machine.
I look at dees Tony an' say to heem: "Wal?"
An' Tony he look back at me an' say: "Hal!
I no can bust up soocha beautiful theeng;
I work weeth my han's eet eet tak' me teell spreeng!"

Antonio Sarto ees buildin' a wall,
But maybe he nevva gon' feenish at all.
Eet sure won'ta be
Teell flower an' tree
An' all kinda growin' theengs sleep een da Fall.

67.   *On the Road to Arden*

AS I went down by Granther's Glade
      Upon the road to Arden,
I stopped to rest me in the shade
   Beside a sunny garden.
So sultry burned the afternoon
The very heavens seemed to swoon;
So still lay all the countryside
That little sounds were magnified;
Behind me, in the hollyhocks,
The bees were loud as chiming clocks!
   I heard them boom:
   "Zoom! zoom! zoom! zoom!"
And long I marveled in the shade
   Beside that sunny garden,
As I went down by Granther's Glade
   Upon the road to Arden.

Upon the little bridge that spanned
   The mill-stream's tinkling water,
I passed the miller's 'prentice and
   The miller's budding daughter.
Her bell-shaped bonnet hid her face;
They stood, removed a little space,
And listless leaned above the weir.
So still! I fancied I could hear—
What else but those same booming clocks,
The loud bees in the hollyhocks?

110

A pulselike beat:
"Sweet! sweet! sweet! sweet!"
Yet listless stood the 'prentice and
  The miller's budding daughter,
Upon the little bridge that spanned
  The mill-stream's tinkling water.

"To find a bonnet, like a bell,
  With a rose face thereunder,
Might fool a bee that loved too well
  His share of sugared plunder."
Thus musing, slow I climbed the hill—
Then, sudden, on the air so still
There burst so sure a booming sound,
I stopped, and quickly turned me round.
A low branch hid the bridge from sight,
And yet—so near! I must be right—
  "Zoom! sweet! zoom! sweet!"
  The notes repeat.
"Some bee," I said, "that loves too well
  His share of sugared plunder,
Has found a bonnet like a bell
  With a rose face thereunder."

68.   *Two Days*

OLD Mike Clancy went for a stroll,
    An' warm an' clear was the sky,
But he came back home with clouds on his soul
    An' a glint o' rain in his eye.

"Och! cold it is out there," sez he;
"The street's no place these days fur me;

Wid motors runnin' through the town
The way they're like to knock ye down,
Wid all the rush an' moidherin' noise,
The impudence of upstart boys;
An' girls, that walk as bold as brass,
An' l'ave small room fur ye to pass.
In twenty blocks, or mebbe more,
I saw no face I'd seen before,
Or care, indeed, to see agen!
W'at's come of all the dacent men,
The kindly friends, I use' to meet
In other days upon the street?
'Tis here at home's the place fur me;
Och! cold it is out there," sez he.

Old Mike Clancy went for a stroll,
    An' cold an' gray was the sky,
But he came back home with warmth in his soul
    An' a glint o' sun in his eye.

"O! sure, this day was fine," sez he,
"An' who d'ye think walked up to me?
A man I thought long dead—Tim Kane!
Och! didn't we talk, there in the rain,
The soft, kind rain we use' to know—
O! not so very long ago—
An' didn't we have a dale to say?
He's eighty-two years old come May—
An' I'm no more than sivinty-nine!
An' didn't he stan' there straight an' fine?
It done me good, the look in his eye,
An' how he laughed an' slapped his thigh;
'I'm good,' sez he, 'fur ten years, too!'
An' faith I do believe it's true.
A man's as old as he feels, d'ye see?—
O! sure, this day was fine," sez he.

GUY WETMORE CARRYL

69. *The Sycophantic Fox and the*
     Gullible Raven

(1873-1904)

A RAVEN sat upon a tree,
    And not a word he spoke, for
His beak contained a piece of Brie,
    Or, maybe, it was Roquefort?
        We'll make it any kind you please—
        At all events, it was a cheese.

Beneath the tree's umbrageous limb
    A hungry fox sat smiling;
He saw the raven watching him,
    And spoke in words beguiling:
        "*J'admire*," said he, "*ton beau plumage*,"
        (The which was simply persiflage).

Two things there are, no doubt you know,
    To which a fox is used,—
A rooster that is bound to crow,
    A crow that's bound to roost,
        And whichsoever he espies
        He tells the most unblushing lies.

"Sweet fowl," he said, "I understand
    You're more than merely natty:
I hear you sing to beat the band
    And Adelina Patti.
        Pray render with your liquid tongue
        A bit from 'Gotterdammerung.'"

This subtle speech was aimed to please
    The crow, and it succeeded:
He thought no bird in all the trees
    Could sing as well as he did.
        In flattery completely doused,
        He gave the "Jewel Song" from "Faust."

But gravitation's law, of course,
   As Isaac Newton showed it,
Exerted on the cheese its force,
   And elsewhere soon bestowed it.
     In fact, there is no need to tell
     What happened when to earth it fell.

I blush to add that when the bird
   Took in the situation,
He said one brief, emphatic word,
   Unfit for publication.
     The fox was greatly startled, but
     He only sighed and answered "Tut!"

THE MORAL is: A fox is bound
   To be a shameless sinner.
And also: When the cheese comes round
   You know it's after dinner.
     But (what is only known to few)
     The fox is after dinner, too.

JAMES J. MONTAGUE

70.   *A Scot's Farewell to his Golf Ball*
                   (1873-)

GUID bye, auld ba'! Fu' mony a year
   I've sent ye sailin' yon an' hither;
But, puir, wee friend, I sairly fear
   We'll play nae mair at gowf thegither.
Ye willna last the summer through,
   As I ha' airnestly been hopin',
For ye are bidin' here the noo,
   A' bruk wide open.

JAMES J. MONTAGUE

I swung at ye wi' micht an' main
 I thocht to send ye fairly flyin',
I didna see the ledge o' stane
 Beneath the sand whaur ye were lyin'.
I was ower hasty, for I meant
 To stand a wee bit closer to ye,
But pressin' juist a mite I sent
 My niblick through ye.

Ye bore fu' mony a dent an' scar,
 An' cut an mashie mairk aboot ye,
But mon! ye'd travel fast an' far
 Whenever I wad brawly cloot ye.
Fu' aft's the time ye've hid yersel
 Amang the gorse an' broom around ye,
But I ha' hunted lang an' well
 An' always found ye.

A bonny time for gowf, the fa'
 But noo—an' sairly I deplore it,
I needs maun buy anither ba'
 An' gi' a precious shillin' for it.
The game is my ane lane delight,
 But it grows costly, past a' reason;—
Puir broken ba', I hoped ye might
 Last oot the season.

JAMES W. FOLEY

71. *Passamquoddy's Apple Toddy*

(1874-   )

PINDAR PEEL, of Passamquoddy,
 Made some birthday apple toddy
An' gits snubbed by everybody
(Female sect) in Passamquoddy.

JAMES W. FOLEY

He put apple brandy in it,
Put hot water in t' thin it,
Stood an hour t' stir an' spin it,
Timed it to th' very minute.

Watched it with th' tenderest feelin',
Knowed it would be soothin', healin',
Grated in some orange peelin'.
Toddy, say! That was a real un.

Pindar Peel, of Passamquoddy,
Sent a bid t' everybody
To jine him in apple toddy,
(Hemale sect) in Passamquoddy.

It had big baked apples floatin'
In it, an' I was a-notin'
Nutmeg smell, an' Peel was totin'
Glasses 'round an' jest a-gloatin'.

Ezry Beggs was thar, an' Struthers,
Homer Blake an' Job Caruthers,
Treadwell Pew an' his two brothers,
Me an' half a dozen others.

We set thar a while a-gassin',
Crackin' jokes an' neighbor-sassin',
An' while toddy was a-passin'
Ye sh'd hear th' tongues unfasten.

Me ner Job ner anybody
Ever drunk sech apple toddy
Made all-wool without no shoddy
In th' days o' Passamquoddy.

Never see sech sly, deceivin'
Stuff as that—past all believin';
Put th' real kibosh on grievin',
Loosed up tongue-tied fellers even.

JAMES W. FOLEY

Homer Blake an' Job Caruthers
Sung some college songs (an' others)
An' Tread Pew an' his two brothers
Danced a Highland fling with Struthers.

It was winter, an' th' wind er-
Roarin', but we all begin ter
Feel th' heat, by jing, an' Pindar
Shoved Gabe Struthers out th' winder!

Then reached out—he seed he'd haf ter
Pull him back—an' give th' gaff ter
Gabe, an' shook so hard with laughter
That he went a-tumblin' after.

Wal, we got 'em back, an' Struthers
Wrastled Treadwell Pew's two brothers,
Blacked an eye fer Job Caruthers,
Skinned my nose an' hurt some others.

But th' was th' best o' feelin'!
Pindar Peel kep' on a-dealin'
Toddy out—put in more peelin'.
Homer Blake nigh kicked th' ceilin'.

Ezry Beggs was that onstable
He slid underneath th' table,
Plumb onstiddy, pitch an' gable,
Tried t' rise, but wasn't able.

Pindar simply kep' th' kittle
Hard a-bile, full to th' middle,
Didn't no one have no tittle
Too much er no jot too little.

JAMES W. FOLEY

Job Caruthers felt like takin'
Jest a little nap; an' makin'
Him a bed, laid down till breakin'
Dawn without no sign o' wakin'.

Pindar Peel took home Gabe Struthers;
Treadwell went with his two brothers,
Hardly knowin' which fr'm t' others,
Which was like me—an' some others.

Nex' day Pindar Heerd fr'm Struthers'
Wife, an' Blake's an' Job Caruthers'
Treadwell Pew's an' his two brothers',
Mine—an' mebbe fr'm some others.

Pindar writ a note an' sent it,
Beggin' pardon—an' he meant it;
Said th' was no harm intended,
Said them apples had fermented.

Treadwell Pew an' his two brothers,
Homer Blake an' Job Caruthers
Took probation—an' Gabe Struthers,
Me an' half a dozen others.

He gits snubbed by everybody
(Female sect) in Passamquoddy,
Jest fer makin' birthday toddy,
Pindar Peel, of Passamquoddy.

WILLIAM F. KIRK

72.   *The Goldfish*   (1877-   )

"TRUE culture is not for the masses,"
    Said Mrs. De Lancy De Vane.
"One has to look up to the classes
    To find the intelligent brain.

WILLIAM F. KIRK

You grasp what I mean. If one travels
  One goes where the leaders are found."
And the goldfish kept swimming around and around
  And the goldfish kept swimming around.

"We people that live in the city
  Find much to deplore, in a way.
At times I can almost feel pity
  For persons that toil by the day.
Those persons in overalls, dearie,
  And those guards in the tubes underground—"
And the goldfish kept swimming around and around
  And the goldfish kept swimming around.

"I feel that my culture compels me
  To live and to move like a queen.
A vague inner consciousness tells me—
  But doubtless you grasp what I mean!
We people of fine birth and breeding
  Are the sort that grow great and renowned—"
And the goldfish stopped swimming around and around
  And the goldfish stopped swimming around!

EDWIN MEADE ROBINSON

73.   *The Story of Ug*

(1878-   )

UG was a hairy but painstaking artist,
    Back in a simple and primitive age.
Listen, young Poet! And ere thou departest,
  Haply thou'lt learn something. (Haply thou'lt
    rage!)

EDWIN MEADE ROBINSON

Ug fashioned arrowheads, slowly and neatly,
Chipping all day at the hardest of stone;
Made them symmetrical, polished them sweetly,
Sharpened their points with a skill all his own.

Long ones and short ones and fat ones or narrow,
Bolts of obsidian, spearheads of flint;
Some that could crash through a mastodon's marrow,
Some that were prized for their beautiful tint;
Endless varieties told of his talents—
All were alike in that all were acute,
All had the symmetry, finish and balance
Arrows must have if one wants them to shoot.

And then, one day,
Ug began to notice
A distinct falling off in his trade,
And, upon inquiry, he found
That a new school of arrowhead-makers
Who made what they called "Free Arrowheads"
Was getting popular among the young men.
The arrowheads were "free"
In the sense that they had no shape,
Being mere amorphous chunks
Of flint, or sandstone or blue mud
Or any thing.
It seems that the old, shapely kind
Was felt to be monotonous and antique,
Being even on both sides,
Like a foolish old Grecian Jar,
Or a butterfly, or a woman.
While the new kind
Could "express the soul" of its maker,
In looking like a piece of cheese.
You couldn't hit anything with the new kind
Because they wouldn't shoot straight;

EDWIN MEADE ROBINSON

But being purely "subjective" arrowheads,
They weren't intended to hit anything.
So Ug was neglected,
Until people began to get hungry . . .
And then, since he was the only
Skilled maker left in the country
He became
A millionaire.

74.   Fishers

SIMON, called Peter, and Andrew his brother,
    And James, son of Zebedee, and his brother John,
  Early in the morning, they hailed one another,
  Starting for the lake before the stars were gone,
Early in the morning, early in the morning,
  Never start a-fishing when the dew gets dry;
Sons of John and Zebedee, on the banks of Galilee,
  There they sat a-fishing when the Lord came by.

Friends he was after, to hold 'em and bind 'em—
  And make 'em all his brothers for his dear name's
    sake;
Loyal men, true men, he knew where to find 'em—
Early in the morning by the dim, blue lake.
Early in the morning, early in the morning.
  When the birds are waking with their hallelujah song,
Men with simple, thankful souls like the larks and
    orioles,
  There they'd be a-fishing when the Lord came along!

Fragrance of mint beds, cooing of the pigeon,
  All the loveliness of earth, from the world with-
    drawn—
I'm afraid the only time I feel a real religion
  Is when God comes walking on the waters with the
    dawn;

Early in the morning, early in the morning,
　By the living waters, I never want to die!
But if He is close at hand, here's the place to meet Him,
　　and
　I want to be a-fishing when my Lord comes by!

75.　　*A Song of the Movie Mexican*

OH, I am a brave desperado,
　　And I wear a wide spreading sombrero;
I am noted for sneers and bravado,
　And I constantly dance the bolero.
I murder the foul renegado,
　And I lose my dinero at faro;
And I lie in a dark ambuscado
　　To capture my rival ranchero.

　　　　　　　　(Cho.)
　　Maraschino!
　　Peperino!
　　Don Pedro and Little Casino!
　　Merino,
　　Tondino—
　　Tortillas and chili and bino!

I run from the brave 'Mericano,
　And I shrink from the soap and sapolio;
I play the guitar and piano,
　And I grease my frijoles with oleo;
I sing the fandango, soprano,
　And I swipe the base Gringo's portfolio;
For I am the Mexican man, O,
　Who appears in each movie embroglio!

　　　　　　(Cho.)
　　Maraschino! etc.

122

DON MARQUIS

76. *Noah an' Jonah an' Cap'n John Smith*

(1878–   )

NOAH an' Jonah an' Cap'n John Smith,
Mariners, travelers, magazines of myth,
Settin' up in Heaven, chewin' and a-chawin'
Eatin' their terbaccy, talkin' and a-jawin';
Settin' by a crick, spittin' in the worter,
Talkin' tall an' tactless, as saints hadn't orter,
Lollin' in the shade, baitin' hooks and anglin',
Occasionally friendly, occasionally wranglin'.

Noah took his halo from his old bald head
An' swatted of a hoppergrass an' knocked it dead,
An' he baited of his hook, an' he spoke an' said:
"When I was the Skipper of the tight leetle Ark
I useter fish fer porpus, useter fish fer shark,
Often I have ketched in a single hour on Monday
Sharks enough to feed the fambly till Sunday—
To feed all the sarpints, the tigers an' donkeys,
To feed all the zebras, the insects an' monkeys,
To feed all the varmints, bears an' gorillars,
To feed all the camels, cats an' armadillers,
To give all the pelicans stews for their gizzards,
To feed all the owls an' catamounts an' lizards,
To feed all the humans, their babies an' their nusses,
To feed all the houn' dawgs an' hippopotamusses,
To feed all the oxens, feed all the asses,
Feed all the bison an' lettle hoppergrasses—
Always I ketched, in half a hour on Monday
All that the fambly could gormandize till Sunday!"

Jonah took his harp, to strum and to string her,
An' Cap'n John Smith teched his nose with his finger.

DON MARQUIS

Cap'n John Smith, he hemmed some an' hawed some,
An' he bit off a chaw, an' he chewed some and chawed
    some:—
"When I was to China, when I was to Guinea,
When I was to Java, an' also in Verginney,
I teached all the natives how to be ambitious,
I learned 'em my trick of ketchin' devilfishes.
I've fitten tigers, I've fitten bears,
I have fitten sarpints an' wolves in their lairs,
I have fit with wild men an' hippopotamusses,
But the perilousest varmints is the bloody octopusses!
I'd rub my forehead with phosphorescent light
An' plunge into the ocean an' seek 'em out at night!
I ketched 'em in grottoes, I ketched 'em in caves,
I used fer to strangle 'em underneath the waves!
When they seen the bright light blazin' on my forehead
They used ter to rush at me, screamin' something
    horrid!
Tentacles wavin', teeth white an' gnashin',
Hollerin' an' bellerin', wallerin' an' splashin'!
I useter grab 'em as they rushed from their grots,
Ketch all their legs an' tie 'em into knots!"

Noah looked at Jonah, an' said not a word,
But if winks made noises, a wink had been heard.
Jonah took the hook from a mudcat's middle
An' strummed on the strings of his hallelujah fiddle;
Jonah give his whiskers a backhand wipe
An' cut some plug terbaccer an' crammed it in his pipe!
—(Noah an' Jonah an' Cap'n John Smith,
Fisherman an' travelers, narreratin' myth,
Settin' up in Heaven all eternity,
Fishin' in the shade, contented as could be!
Spittin' their terbaccer in the little shaded creek,
Stoppin' of their yarns fer ter hear the ripples speak!

DON MARQUIS

I hope fer Heaven, when I think of this—
You folks bound hellward, a lot of fun you'll miss!)

Jonah, he decapitates that mudcat's head,
An' gets his pipe ter drawin'; an' this is what he said:
"Excuse me ef your stories don't excite me much!
Excuse me ef I seldom agitate fer such!
You think yer fishermen! I won't argue none!
I won't even tell yer the half o' what I done!
You has careers dangerous an' checkered!
All as I will say is: Go and read my record!
You think yer fishermen! You think yer great!
All I asks is this: Has one of ye been *'bait?*
Cap'n Noah, Cap'n John, I heerd when ye hollered;
What I asks is this: Has one of ye been *swallered?*
It's mighty purty fishin' with little hooks an' reels.
It's mighty easy fishin' with little rods an' creels.
It's mighty pleasant ketchin' mudcats fer yer dinners.
But this here is my challenge fer saints an' fer sinners,
Which one of ye has v'yaged in a varmint's inners?
When I seen a big fish, tough as Methooslum,
I used for to dive into his oozly-goozlum!
When I seen the strong fish, wallopin' like a lummicks,
I useter foller 'em, dive into their stummicks!
I could v'yage an' steer 'em, I could understand 'em,
I useter navigate 'em, I useter land 'em!
Don't you pester *me* with any more narration!
Go git famous! Git a reputation!"

—Cap'n John he grinned his hat brim beneath,
Clicked his tongue of silver on his golden teeth:
Noah an' Jonah an' Cap'n John Smith,
Strummin' golden harps, narreratin' myth!
Settin' by the shallows forever an' forever,
Swappin' yarns an' fishin' in a little river!

77.   *A Tragedy of the Deep*

THOUGHT may, at times, be a very dangerous
      thing . . .
It is better never to use conscious thought
Until instinct has flivvered.
There was once an Octopus
Who was very proud of his eight legs . . .
They were long and slithery and beautiful,
And he would sit on his ear
And wave them in front of his face in the water
And admire them by the hour.
A Shark, who had no legs or tentacles at all,
Used to watch the Octopus,
And he grew weary of the Octopus's self-content . .
One day, with a most malicious intention,
The Shark said to the Octopus:
"Your tentacles, or legs, or whatever you call them,
Are very pretty indeed:
And it pleases me to observe your continuing enthu-
      siasm with regard to them . . .
I have never seen you swim . . .
May I ask you, when you swim, which leg do you
      wiggle first?—
The right-hand leg in front?
The right-hand leg behind?
The right-hand leg in front of the right-hand leg
      behind?
Or the right-hand leg behind the front right-hand leg?
Or do you begin with one of the left-hand legs?"
The Octopus said: "Why, I start with . . . "
And then he stopped . . .
He had always swum before without thinking . . .
He had always swum by instinct . . .
How *did* he start?

DON MARQUIS

With the front leg on the left-hand side?
Or the front leg on the right-hand side?
For the life of him he couldn't remember . . .
He tried one set of legs, and it didn't seem the proper
way;
And he tried another set, and *they* weren't the right
ones . . .
And he stopped trying and thought and thought and
thought . . .
And the more he thought the less able he was to swim
at all.
To draw this painful story to a conclusion at once,
The Octopus sat in the midst of his legs
Looking wanly at the subaqueous world
Until he starved to death
Through his inability to catch food.
The moral is, *Never think as long as you can dodge
thought.*

THEODOSIA GARRISON

78.   *Himself*

THE houseful that we were then, you could count
us by the dozens,
The wonder was that sometimes the old walls
wouldn't burst;
Herself (the Lord be good to her!), the aunts and rafts
of cousins,
The young folks and the children—but Himself
came first.

Master of the House he was, and well for them that
    know it;
  His cheeks like winter apples and his head like snow;
Eyes as blue as water when the sun of March shines
    through it,
  An' steppin' like a soldier with his stick held so.

Faith, but he could tell a tale would serve a man for
    wages,
  Sing a song would put the joy of dancin' in two
    sticks;
But saints between themselves and harm that saw him
    in his rages,
  Blazin' and oratin' over chess and politics.

Master of the House he was, and that beyond all sayin',
  Eh, the times I've heard him exhortin' from his chair
The like of any Bishop, yet snappin' off his prayin'
  To put the curse on Phelan's dog for howlin' in the
    prayer.

The times I've seen him walkin' out like Solomon in
    glory,
  Salutin' with great elegance the gentry he might
    meet;
An eye for every pretty girl, an ear for every story,
  And takin' as his just deserts the middle of the street.

Master of the House—with much to love and be for-
    given,
  Yet, thinkin' of Himself today—Himself—I see
    him go
With that old light step of his across the Courts of
    Heaven,
  His hat a little sideways and his stick held so.

128

THOMAS YBARRA

79.　　　*Lay of Ancient Rome*

(1880-　　)

OH, the Roman was a rogue,
　　He erat was, you bettum;
He ran his automobilis
　　And smoked his cigarettum;
He wore a diamond studibus
　　And elegant cravattum,
A maxima cum laude shirt,
　　And such a stylish hattum!

He loved the luscious hic-hæc-hoc,
　　And bet on games and equi;
At times he won; at others, though,
　　He got it in the nequi;
He winked (quo usque tandem?)
　　At puellas on the Forum,
And sometimes even made
　　Those goo-goo oculorum!

He frequently was seen
　　At combats gladiatorial,
And ate enough to feed
　　Ten boarders at Memorial;
He often went on sprees
　　And said, on starting homus,
"Hic labor—opus est,
　　Oh, where's my hic—hic—domus?"

Although he lived in Rome—
　　Of all the arts the middle—
He was (excuse the phrase)
　　A horrid individ'l;
Ah! what a different thing
　　Was the homo (dative, hominy)
Of far away B. C.
　　From us of Anno Domini.

129

FRANKLIN PIERCE ADAMS

80.   *To His Lyre*
                                         (1881–   )
AD LYRAM
Horace; Book 1, Ode 32
"Poscimur. Si quid vacui sub umbra—"

IF EVER, as I struck thy strings,
   I've sounded one enduring note,
Let me, O Lyre, think up some things
   That folks will simply have to quote.

A Lesbian lyrist owned thee once;
   He used to sing a lot, he did,
Of dames and demijohns and stunts
   Like that. He was the Tuneful Kid.

Help me, mine ancient ukulele,
   Sing songs of sorrow and of joy,
Such as, composed and printed daily,
   Will make the public yell, "Oh, *boy!*"

81.   *Jim and Bill*

BILL JONES was cynical and sad;
   He thought sincerity was rare;
Most people, Bill believed, were bad
   And few were fair.

He said that cheating was the rule;
   That nearly everything was fake;
That nearly all, both knave and fool,
   Were on the make.

Jim Brown was cheerful as the sun;
   He thought the world a lovely place,
Exhibiting to every one
   A smiling face.

130

FRANKLIN PIERCE ADAMS

He thought that every man was fair;
    He had no cause to sob or sigh;
He said that everything was square
    As any die.

Dear reader, would you rather be
    Like Jim, not crediting the ill,
Joyous in your serenity,
    Or right, like Bill?

82.   *Metaphysics*

A MAN morose and dull and sad—
    Go ask him why he feels so bad.
Behold! He answers it is drink
That put his nerves upon the blink.

Another man whose smile and jest
Disclose a nature of the best—
What keeps his heart and spirits up?
Again we learn it is the cup.

The moral to this little bit
Is anything you make of it.
Such recondite philosophy
Is far away too much for me.

BERTON BRALEY

83.   *Pan in Pandemonium*
                                        (1882–   )
PAN went dancing up and down the city
    No one saw him, cloven-hoofed and brown,
Pan went piping where the streets were gritty
    But his notes were swallowed in the roar of town.

BERTON BRALEY

Yet Pan's long ears were attuned to listen
    And Pan heard whispers of the old Romance,
And Pan's bright eyes seemed to gleam and glisten,
    And there was laughter in his pagan glance.

For Pan saw lovers where the Park paths wander,
    And Pan saw lovers when the busses passed,
And Pan heard voices that grew sweeter, fonder,
    On the wires that bind us in a network vast.

And Pan saw beauty that was Greek and slender,
    And Pan heard kisses in the hall-ways dim,
And Pan saw glances that were blithe and tender,
    So the cruel city couldn't hoodwink him!

Pan wasn't cozened by the jazz and clamor
    Wise and canny was the slim brown god,
Pan found the city full of love's glad glamor
    And danced back gaily to his sylvan sod!

JOYCE KILMER

84.   *A Blue Valentine*

           For Aline

                                    (1886–1918)

MONSIGNORE,
        Right Reverend Bishop Valentinus,
Sometime of Interamna, which is called Ferni,
Now of the delightful Court of Heaven,
I respectfully salute you,
I genuflect
And I kiss your episcopal ring.

It is not, Monsignore,
The fragrant memory of your holy life,

JOYCE KILMER

Nor that of your shining and joyous martyrdom,
Which causes me now to address you.
But since this is your august festival, Monsignore,
It seems appropriate to me to state
According to a venerable and agreeable custom,
That I love a beautiful lady.
Her eyes, Monsignore,
Are so blue that they put lovely little blue reflections
On everything that she looks at,
Such as a wall
Or the moon
Or my heart.
It is like the light coming through blue stained glass,
Yet not quite like it,
For the blueness is not transparent,
Only translucent.
Her soul's light shines through,
But her soul cannot be seen.
It is something elusive, whimsical, tender, wanton,
   infantile, wise
And noble.
She wears, Monsignore, a blue garment,
Made in the manner of the Japanese.
It is very blue—
I think that her eyes have made it more blue,
Sweetly staining it
As the pressure of her body has graciously given it
   form.
Loving her, Monsignore,
I love all her attributes;
But I believe
That even if I did not love her
I would love the blueness of her eyes,
And her blue garment, made in the manner of the
   Japanese.

JOYCE KILMER

Monsignore,
I have never before troubled you with a request.
The saints whose ears I chiefly worry with my pleas
    are the most exquisite and maternal Brigid,
Gallant Saint Stephen, who puts fire in my blood,
And your brother bishop, my patron,
The generous and jovial Saint Nicholas of Bari.
But, of your courtesy, Monsignore,
Do me this favour:
When you this morning make your way
To the Ivory Throne that bursts into bloom with roses
    because of her who sits upon it,
When you come to pay your devoir to Our Lady,
I beg you, say to her:
"Madame, a poor poet, one of your singing servants
    yet on earth,
Has asked me to say that at this moment he is especially
    grateful to you
For wearing a blue gown."

85.   *Servant Girl and Grocer's Boy*

HER lips' remark was: "Oh, you kid!"
    Her soul spoke thus (I know it did):

"O king of realms of endless joy,
My own, my golden grocer's boy,

I am a princess forced to dwell
Within a lonely kitchen cell,

While you go dashing through the land
With loveliness on every hand.

Your whistle strikes my eager ears
Like music of the choiring spheres.

134

JOYCE KILMER

The mighty earth grows faint and reels
Beneath your thundering wagon wheels.

How keenly, perilously sweet
To cling upon that swaying seat!

How happy she who by your side
May share the splendors of that ride!

Ah, if you will not take my hand
And bear me off across the land,

Then, traveller from Arcady,
Remain awhile and comfort me.

What other maiden can you find
So young and delicate and kind?"

Her lips' remark was: "Oh, you kid!"
Her soul spoke thus (I know it did).

ALINE KILMER

86.   *Ambition*

KENTON and Deborah, Michael and Rose,
These are fine children as all the world knows;
But into my arms in my dreams every night
Come Peter and Christopher, Faith and Delight.

Kenton is tropical, Rose is pure white,
Deborah shines like a star in the night;
Michael's round eyes are as blue as the sea,
And nothing on earth could be dearer to me.

But where is the baby with Faith can compare?
What is the colour of Peterkin's hair?
Who can make Christopher clear to my sight,
Or show me the eyes of my daughter Delight?

ALINE KILMER

When people inquire I always just state:
"I have four nice children and hope to have eight.
Though the first four are pretty and certain to please,
Who knows but the rest may be nicer than these?"

WILLIAM ROSE BENET

87.   *Debutantrum*

(1886–   )

O PANSY-EYE, O polished face,
  O spring enchanted feline,
You who the *haute couture* would grace
  With duds from neck to kneeline—

The birds are in the park, my girl,
  The buds are busting sure,
A sports hat of *rose visca perle*
  Adorns your sleek coiffure.

Draining dark coffee to the lees
  I hunch at lunch in Mendel's.
You toy with sole at Marguery's,
  Fare forth to shop at Bendel's.

Eftsoons, of course, some gilded loon
  Will make you fervent promises,
And Mendelssohn will call the tune
  To crowds within St. Thomas's.

Yet, meanwhile, gal, I'll say you shock
  My heart to a hosanna
In that new Premet jumper-frock
  Or smoking-suit from Anna.

I love you in that Lanvin cape,
  Those Chanel togs, my Nora,

WILLIAM ROSE BENET

And when you pass in Roman crepe
I doff my nicked fedora.

So, lovely Molyneux mirage,
With many a *chic* and chaste line,
In smart deep V *decolletage*
Or sinuous slanting waist line,

Hark, hark! My funds would never reach
To Paris or the Lido:
I could not squire you to Palm Beach,
White Sulphur or Tuxedo;

But, if you feel a man's a man
(To swat you with a spanner),
I know an easy-payment plan;
We'd live at Bellerose Manor.

With joy I'd then commute, you bet.
We'd pluck spring flowers all pollenny;
You'd dominate the junior set
In some suburban colony.

Don't laugh! But, no—your laugh rings free,
You shriek—you toss your tresses.
Farewell! Some day you'll merely be
"Among the patronesses"!

CHRISTOPHER MORLEY

(1890-   )

88.   *A Hallowe'en Memory*

DO you remember, Heart's Desire,
    The night when Hallowe'en first came?
The newly dedicated fire,
    The hearth unsanctified by flame?

CHRISTOPHER MORLEY

How anxiously we swept the bricks
   (How tragic, were the draught not right!)
And then the blaze enwrapped the sticks
   And filled the room with dancing light.

We could not speak, but only gaze,
   Nor half believe what we had seen—
Our home, *our* hearth, *our* golden blaze,
   Our cider mugs, *our* Hallowe'en!

And then a thought occurred to me—
   We ran outside with sudden shout
And looked up at the roof, to see
   Our own dear smoke come drifting out.

And of all man's felicities
   The very subtlest one, say I,
Is when, for the first time, he sees
   His hearthfire smoke against the sky.

Translations from the Chinese

89.   POETS EASILY CONSOLED

THE anguishes of poets are
   Less grim than other men's, by far:
When other men can only curse,
The poet puts his woes in verse.
And Yee Lee, though at first the pang was smart
When by his friend Wu Wu his bride was stolen,
Soon asked which best expressed a broken heart,
A dash, a comma, or a semi-colon?

138

90.   DENY YOURSELF

IF YOU haven't any ideas
    Don't worry.
You can get along without them—
Many of the nicest people do.

91.   THE CODE

THOSE fireflies sparkling in the willows,
    Here, there, here, there;
Those frogs piping in the moonlit pond,
Tweedle, tweedle, tweedle—
There seems to be a persistent method in it.
What is the code?
Is Nature trying to get across some message to me?

92.   *My Pipe*

MY PIPE is old
    And caked with soot;
My wife remarks:
"How can you put
That horrid relic,
So unclean,
Inside your mouth?
The nicotine
Is strong enough
To stupefy
A Swedish plumber."
I reply:

"This is the kind
Of pipe I like:
I fill it full
Of Happy Strike,

CHRISTOPHER MORLEY

Or Barking Cat
Or Cabman's Puff,
Or Brooklyn Bridge
(That potent stuff)
Or Chaste Embraces,
Knacker's Twists,
Old Honeycomb
Or Niggerfist.

"I clamp my teeth
Upon its stem—
It is my bliss,
My diadem.
Whatever Fate
May do to me,
This is my favorite
B.
B B.
For this dear pipe
You feign to scorn
I smoked the night
The boy was born."

ELINOR WYLIE

93.   *The Poor Old Cannon*

UPBROKE the sun
  In red-gold foam;
Thus spoke the gun
At the Soldiers' Home:

"Whenever I hear
Blue thunder speak
My voice sounds clear,
But little and weak.

ELINOR WYLIE

"And when the proud
Young cockerels crow
My voice sounds loud,
But gentle and low.

"When the mocking-bird
Prolongs his note
I cannot be heard
Though I split my throat."

94.   *Little Joke*

STRIPPING an almond tree in flower
    The wise apothecary's skill
A single drop of lethal power
    From perfect sweetness can distil.

From bitterness in efflorescence,
    With murderous poisons packed therein,
The poet draws pellucid essence
    Pure as a drop of metheglin.

INDEX OF AUTHORS

143

INDEX OF TITLES

145

INDEX OF TITLES

146

INDEX OF TITLES

INDEX OF FIRST LINES

INDEX OF FIRST LINES

INDEX OF FIRST LINES